Global Wage Report 2012/13

Wages and equitable growth

International Labour Organization

The International Labour Organization (ILO) was founded in 1919 to promote social justice and thereby contribute to universal and lasting peace. The ILO is responsible for drawing up and overseeing international labour standards. It is the only tripartite United Nations agency that brings together representatives of governments, employers and workers to jointly shape policies and programmes promoting Decent Work for all. This unique arrangement gives the ILO an edge in incorporating 'real world' knowledge about employment and work.

Global Wage Report 2012/13

Wages and equitable growth

International Labour Office · Geneva
Academic Foundation · New Delhi

First published in 2013 by

International Labour Office,
CH-1211 Geneva 22, Switzerland
www.ilo.org

in association with

Academic Foundation
(co-publication partners for South Asia)
4772/23 Bharat Ram Road, (23 Ansari Road), Darya Ganj,
New Delhi - 110002, India.
www.academicfoundation.com

Global Wage Report 2012/13: Wages and equitable growth
Geneva, International Labour Office, 2013

wages / minimum wage / employment / unemployment / household income / labour productivity / economic recession / developed countries / developing countries
13.07

ISBN 978-92-2-126237-4 (PDF)

Also available in PDF in Arabic: ISBN 978-92-2-626237-9; Chinese: ISBN 978-92-2-526237-0; French: ISBN 978-92-2-226237-3; Portuguese: ISBN 978-92-2-826237-7; Russian: ISBN 978-92-2-426237-1; Spanish: ISBN 978-92-2-326237-2.

Also available as EPUB in English: ISBN 978-92-2-126923-6; French: ISBN 978-92-2-226923-5; and Spanish: ISBN 978-92-2-326923-4. Also available in Kindle and iBook edition.

ILO Cataloguing in Publication Data

ISBN 978-81-7188-996-9 (Academic Foundation / for South Asia)

Digitally produced from DocBook XML files by Corbas Ltd.

Printed and bound in India.

Preface

The global crisis has had significant negative repercussions for labour markets in many parts of the world, and recovery is proving uncertain and elusive. At the global level, average wages have grown but at lower rates than before the crisis. However this *Global Wage Report 2012/13* shows that the impact of the crisis on wages was far from uniform.

In developed economies, the crisis led to a "double dip" in wages: real average wages fell in 2008 and again in 2011, and the current outlook suggests that in many of these countries wages are growing marginally, if at all, in 2012.

In emerging regions, wage growth has generally been more resilient, with strong growth in Asia and more modest but still positive trends in Africa, Latin America and the Caribbean.

In Eastern Europe and Central Asia the crisis led to falling wages in 2009, with a return to positive but relatively lower wage growth since then.

Taking a longer view, the report estimates that real monthly average wages almost doubled in Asia between 2000 and 2011, and increased by 18 per cent in Africa, 15 per cent in Latin America and the Caribbean, and 5 per cent in developed economies. In Eastern Europe and Central Asia wages nearly tripled, but from a very low base following the economic collapse of the 1990s. In the Middle East, the availability of wage data is limited. What evidence is available indicates that low productivity and weak institutions have kept wages stagnant over the last decade.

This *Global Wage Report* presents data on trends in wages around the world and compares them with trends in labour productivity, analysing their complex effects on the global economy with a view to shedding some light on the current debates over distribution, competitiveness and labour costs. When wages rise in line with productivity increases they are both sustainable and create a stimulus for further economic growth by increasing households' purchasing power. However for a decade or more before the crisis, the link between wages and labour productivity was broken in many countries and this contributed to the creation of global economic imbalances. The report shows that since the 1980s a majority of countries have experienced a downward trend in the "labour income share", which means that a lower share of national income has gone into labour compensation and a higher share into capital incomes. This has happened most frequently where wages have stagnated but also in some countries where real wages have grown strongly. On a social and political level this trend risks creating perceptions that workers and their families are not receiving their fair share of the wealth they create. On an economic level, it could endanger the pace and sustainability of future economic growth by constraining wage-based household consumption. This is particularly true where the era of debt-based consumption has now led to an extended period in which households must pay off earlier debts.

At the global level, while some countries can run a trade surplus or export their way out of recession, this must come at the expense of deficits in importing countries and relocation of jobs. To avoid beggar-thy-neighbour competition, the path to sustained and balanced economic growth must come through increased domestic consumption in surplus countries, based on wages that grow in line with productivity. International coordination can contribute to achieving equitable outcomes that benefit all countries.

Many countries in the world are trying to address these challenges, often by implementing innovative policies. I hope this *Global Wage Report* will help them and will stimulate fresh thinking on issues which today stand at the centre of international decision-making.

Guy Ryder
ILO Director-General

Contents

Part III Implications for equitable growth

Appendices

Tables

Figures

Box

Appendix figure

Appendix boxes

Appendix tables

The ILO Global Wage Database is available at: www.ilo.org/wage12.

Scan the QR code with your smartphone to access the ILO Global Wage Database website.

Acknowledgements

Main contributors

The report was prepared by staff of the Conditions of Work and Employment Branch (TRAVAIL) of the ILO with contributions from colleagues in other ILO departments in Geneva and field offices, under the responsibility of Philippe Marcadent, Director of TRAVAIL. The principal editor of the report was Patrick Belser. The report is the result of teamwork between Patrick Belser, Malte Luebker, Sangheon Lee, Andrés Marinakis, Kristen Sobeck, Daniel Vaughan-Whitehead, Jacobo Velasco and Rosalia Vazquez-Alvarez. Excellent research assistance was provided by Rengin Gunaydin and Mila Daskalova. Kristen Sobeck managed the Global Wage Database and created figures for Part I. Malte Luebker reviewed the global and regional estimates. Rosalia Vazquez-Alvarez provided inputs on wage policies in the Middle East and reviewed Part II of the report. Charlotte Beauchamp coordinated editing and publication. Christian Olsen designed the cover page.

Specific contributions

Part II of the report is based on a research project on 'The macroeconomic analysis of wages' coordinated by Sangheon Lee (ILO, TRAVAIL). The project included contributions from Özlem Onaran (University of Westminster), Giorgos Galanis (University of Westminster and University of Warwick), Marc Lavoie (University of Ottawa), Engelbert Stockhammer (Kingston University), Eckhard Hein (Berlin School of Economics and Law), Matthias Mund (Berlin School of Economics and Law), Servaas Storm (Delft University of Technology), C.W.M. Naastepad (Delft University of Technology), Till Van Treeck (Macroeconomic Policy Institute Düsseldorf) and Simon Sturn (University of Massachusetts Amherst). The project also benefited from inputs from Massimiliano La Marca (ILO, Policy Integration).

Special thanks

Our special thanks go to the whole team of the ILO/SIALC (Information System and Labour Analysis) in Panama, in particular Bolívar Pino, for providing wage data on Latin America and the Caribbean, as well as to Steven Kapsos, for providing the analysis on poverty among wage and salaried workers.

We also would like to thank the following people for their precious input and comments: Janine Berg, Fabio Bertranou, Evangelia Bourmpoula, Monica Castillo,

Juan Chacaltana, Matthieu Charpe, Miguel del Cid, Maria Crisetti, Mauricio Dierckxsens, Chris Edgar, Philippe Egger, Lawrence Egulu, Ekkehard Ernst, Verónica Escudero, Regina Galhardi, Werner Garate, Najati Ghosheh, David Glejberman, Stefan Kühn, Sameer Khatiwada, David Kucera, Bob Kyloh, Chang-Hee Lee, Elva Lopez Mourelo, Moazam Mahmood, Anne Posthuma, Stephen Pursey, Uma Rani, John Ritchotte, Catherine Saget, Reynold Simons, Vincenzo Spiezia, Steven Tobin, Manuela Tomei, Raymond Torres, Geir Tonstol, Zafiris Tzannatos, María Elena Valenzuela, Sher Verick, and four anonymous peer reviewers.

Executive summary

Major trends in wages

The crisis continues to dampen wages

Real average wage growth has remained far below pre-crisis levels globally, going into the red in developed economies, although it has remained significant in emerging economies. Monthly average wages adjusted for inflation – known as real average wages – grew globally by 1.2 per cent in 2011, down from 2.1 per cent in 2010 and 3 per cent in 2007. Because of its size and strong economic performance, China weighs heavily in this global calculation. Omitting China, global real average wages grew at only 0.2 per cent in 2011, down from 1.3 per cent in 2010 and 2.3 per cent in 2007 (see figure 3).

Regional differences in wage growth

There are major geographic variations in the trends in real average wage growth (see figure 7). Wages suffered a double dip in developed economies but remained positive throughout the crisis in Latin America and the Caribbean, and even more so in Asia. Fluctuations were widest in Eastern Europe and Central Asia, partly as a result of the strong post-transition recovery in wages before the global economic crisis, and the severe contraction in real wages in 2009. In the Middle East, real average wages appear to have declined since 2008, but some of the estimates still remain tentative, as they are for Africa.

Cumulative wage growth by region

Differences between the regions are particularly stark if we look at the cumulative wage growth from 2000 to 2011. Globally, real monthly average wages grew by just under a quarter, in Asia they almost doubled, while in the developed world they increased by about 5 per cent. In Eastern Europe and Central Asia real wages nearly tripled, but this was mostly as part of the recovery from the transition to market economies. In Russia, for example, the real value of wages collapsed to less than 40 per cent of their value in the 1990s and it took another decade before wages recovered to their initial level.

Regional differences in wage levels

While wages grew significantly in emerging economies, differences in wage levels remain considerable. In the Philippines, a worker in the manufacturing sector took home around US$1.40 for each hour worked. In Brazil, the hourly direct pay in the sector was US$5.40, in Greece it was US$13.00, in the United States US$23.30 and in Denmark US$34.80 (2010 exchange rates, rounded).

Falling labour shares and equitable growth

A smaller piece of the pie for workers across the world

Between 1999 and 2011 average labour productivity in developed economies increased more than twice as much as average wages (see figure 11). In the United States, real hourly labour productivity in the non-farm business sector increased by about 85 per cent since 1980, while real hourly compensation increased by only around 35 per cent. In Germany, labour productivity surged by almost a quarter over the past two decades while real monthly wages remained flat.

The global trend has resulted in a change in the distribution of national income, with the workers' share decreasing while capital income shares increase in a majority of countries. Even in China, a country where wages roughly tripled over the last decade, GDP increased at a faster rate than the total wage bill – and hence the labour share went down.

The drop in the labour share is due to technological progress, trade globalization, the expansion of financial markets, and decreasing union density, which have eroded the bargaining power of labour. Financial globalization, in particular, may have played a bigger role than previously thought.

The effects of a declining labour share

A decrease in the labour share not only affects perceptions of what is fair – particularly given the growing concerns about excessive pay among CEOs and in the financial sector – it also hurts household consumption and can thus create shortfalls in the aggregate demand. These shortfalls in some countries have been compensated by increasing their net exports, but not all countries can run a current account surplus at the same time. Hence, a strategy of cutting unit labour costs, a frequent policy recommendation for crisis countries with current account deficits, may run the risk of depressing domestic consumption more than it increases exports. If competitive wage cuts are pursued simultaneously in a large number of countries, this may lead to a "race to the bottom" in labour shares, shrinking aggregate demand.

Implications for equitable growth

Income distribution and wage levels

The *Global Wage Report* contributes to a wider literature on the changes in the distribution and levels of wages within and across countries, as well as on the economic and social implications of these trends. One of the key findings of this literature is the growing inequality in income, in terms of functional and personal income distribution.

In terms of functional income distribution, which concerns how national income has been distributed between labour and capital, there is a long run trend towards a falling share of wages and a rising share of profits in many countries. The personal distribution of wages has also become more unequal, with a growing gap between the top 10 per cent and the bottom 10 per cent of wage earners. These internal "imbalances" have tended to create or exacerbate external imbalances, even before the Great Recession, with countries trying to compensate the adverse effects of lower wage shares on consumption demands through easy credit or export surpluses.

Better linking productivity and wages

What should be done? Our analysis suggests that policy actions towards "rebalancing" should be taken at both national and global levels. In attempting to redress external imbalances, policy-makers should refrain from a simplistic view that countries can "cut" their way out of the recession. Policy-makers should pursue policies that promote a close connection between the growth of labour productivity and the growth of workers compensation. The existence of large current-account surplus in some countries suggest that there is room to better link productivity increases and wages as a means to stimulate domestic demand. Policy-makers should be careful not to promote a race to the bottom in labour shares in deficit countries or throughout the Eurozone. Austerity measures that are imposed from the outside and bypass social partners harm effective labour relations.

Strengthening institutions

"Internal rebalancing" can begin by strengthening institutions for wage determination. Given the difficulty with organizing workers, particularly in the context of increasing labour market segmentation and rapid technological changes, more supporting and enabling environments need to be created for collective bargaining. Low-paid workers also need stronger protection in wage determination. Minimum wages, if properly designed, have proved an effective policy tool which can provide a decent wage floor and thus secure a minimum living standard for these workers and their families.

Reforms outside the scope of the labour market

It is unrealistic to try to achieve income distribution solely through labour market policies. Redistribution will also require a number of changes that lie outside of the scope of labour markets, including reform and repair of financial markets to restore their role in channelling resources into productive and sustainable investments. There are other critical dimensions of "rebalancing" which deserve a more detailed analysis, including the balance between taxation of capital and labour incomes.

Looking beyond wage earners

In developing economies, employment guarantee schemes that pay minimum wages are ways to create incentives for private firms to comply with the minimum wage. But because in developing and emerging countries only about half of all workers are wage earners, additional measures are needed to create more wage jobs and to raise the productivity and earnings of those in self-employment.

Raising average labour productivity remains a key challenge which must involve efforts to raise the level of education and the capabilities that are required for productive transformation and economic development. The development of well-designed social protection systems would allow workers and their families to reduce the amounts of precautionary savings, to invest in the education of their children, and to contribute towards stronger domestic consumption demand and raise living standards.

PART I Major trends in wages

1 The global economic context: Crisis, recession and employment

1.1 Economic growth rates vary widely by region

After a period of robust economic growth in the early years of the twenty-first century, the world economy contracted in 2009 as a result of the global financial and economic crisis (see figure 1). The impact of the crisis has been felt very diversely across the globe. In the group of more developed economies, 2009 came to be seen as the year of the "Great Recession", the most severe economic downturn since the "Great Depression" of the 1930s. While the recovery in 2010 was initially stronger than expected, the sovereign debt crisis and the various austerity measures that accompanied it led to a significant deceleration of growth thereafter, particularly in Europe. The group of emerging markets and developing countries, by contrast, avoided a generalized recession and has succeeded in maintaining higher growth rates than developed economies since the year 2000.

Figure 1 Annual average economic growth, 1995–2012 (GDP in constant prices)

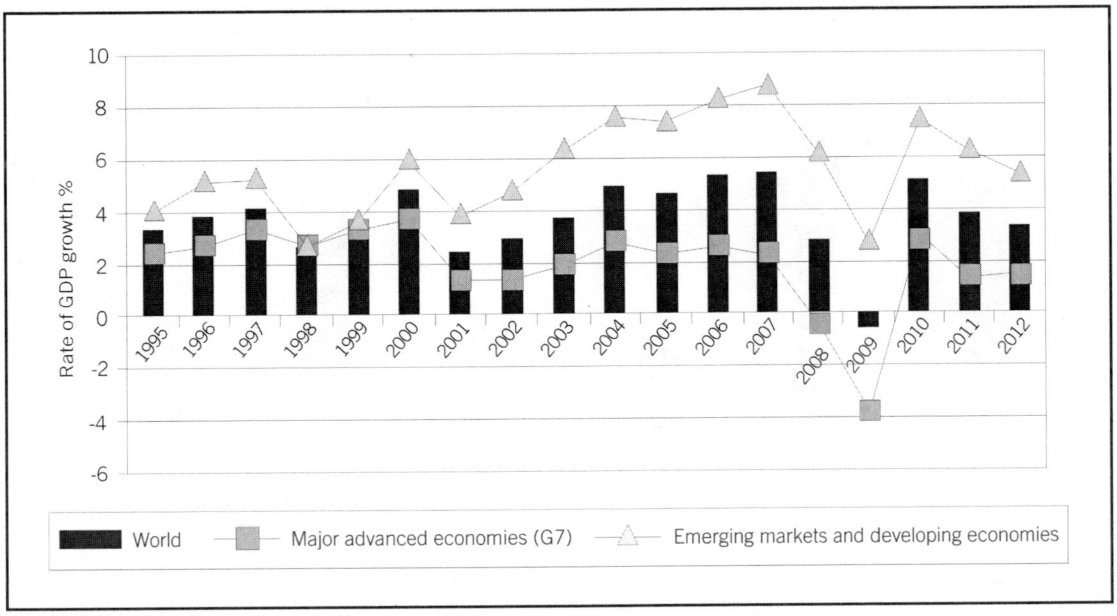

Note: Country groups are those used by the IMF and described in the appendix of IMF, 2012b. Major advanced economies include Canada, France, Germany, Italy, Japan, the United Kingdom and the United States. Emerging markets and developing economies comprise a group of 151 economies that are not classified as advanced economies. Figures for 2012 are projections.

Source: IMF World Economic Outlook database.

Figure 2 Total unemployment rates in the world and in developed economies, 2005–11 (as % of labour force)

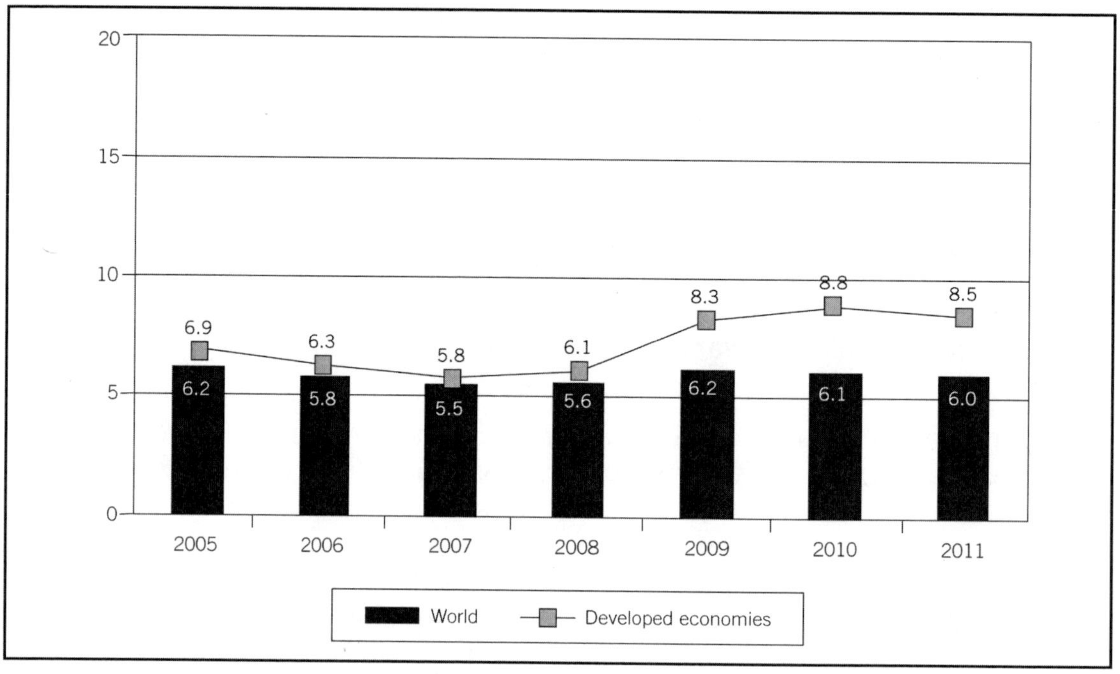

Note: Figures for 2011 are preliminary estimates. For the definition of "developed economies", see Appendix I.
Source: ILO, 2012a.

Figure 3 Annual average global real wage growth, 2006–11

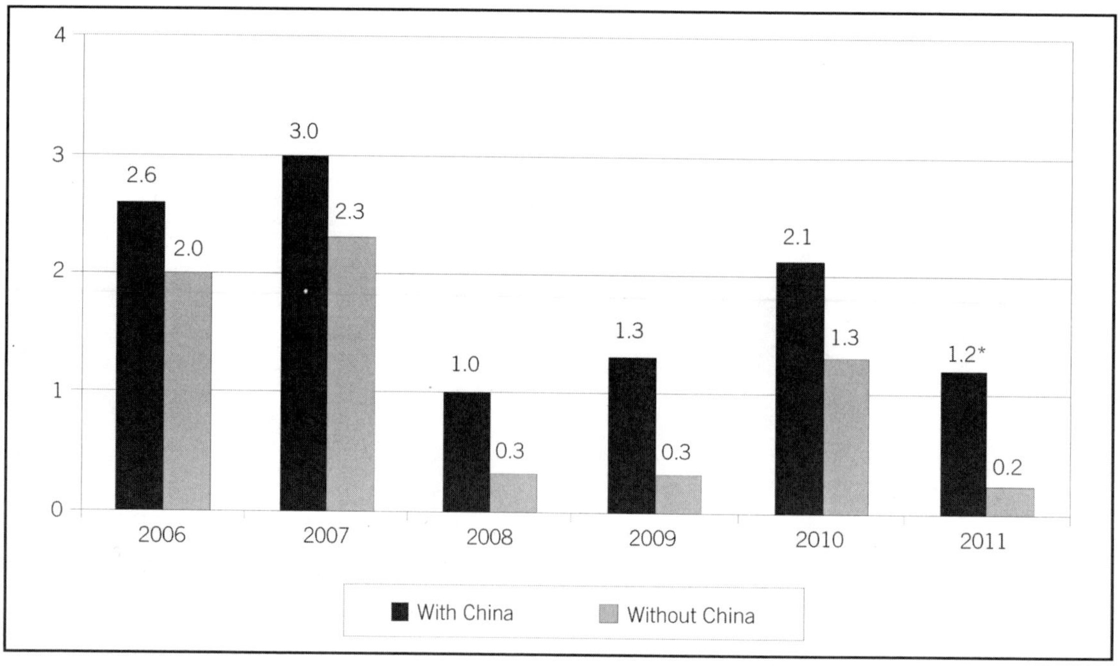

* Growth rates published as "provisional estimates" (based on coverage of *c.* 75%).
Note: Global wage growth is calculated as a weighted average of year-on-year growth in real average monthly wages in 124 countries, covering 94.3 per cent of all employees in the world (for a description of the methodology, see Appendix I).
Source: ILO Global Wage Database.

1.2 Global unemployment rates remain high

The impact of the global financial and economic crisis on labour markets has often been analysed through the prism of the unemployment rate, particularly in developed economies, where unemployment rose from less than 6 per cent to more than 8 per cent of the labour force, with double-digit figures in Greece, Ireland, Portugal and Spain for example.[1] In developing countries unemployment rates fluctuated less. Even so, worldwide unemployment has increased by 27 million since the start of the crisis, bringing the overall number of unemployed to about 200 million or 6 per cent of the global labour force (figure 2). Perhaps the most serious concern relates to youth unemployment, which has reached alarming proportions. The ILO estimates that in 2011 unemployment affected 75 million young people aged 15–24 worldwide, representing more than 12 per cent of all young people. Many more do not appear in the unemployment statistics because they have become so discouraged as to have stopped looking for work.

2 Real average wages

2.1 Slowing growth across a varied landscape

Global estimates of real average wage growth

Employment and unemployment figures do not tell the full story of the impact of the crisis on labour markets. The present report looks at the wages of paid employees.[2] The main unit of measure used for wages is the monthly average wage, rather than hourly or daily wages, expressed in real terms (i.e. adjusted for inflation), which has been identified as an ILO "decent work indicator".[3] Trends in real average monthly wage reflect changes in average labour income (before taxes and transfers) and hence provide a clearer picture of variations in the purchasing power of wages. As will be discussed in the next sections of the report, trends in real average wages vary across regions and countries. Yet the impact of the crisis is clearly noticeable at the aggregate level. Figure 3 reveals that for the last four successive years (from 2008 to 2011), the growth in real monthly average wages remained positive but has fallen to well below pre-crisis rates. This is true whether or not we include official wage statistics from China, although omitting China from the analysis significantly reduces global wage growth, given the country's large size (in terms of number of wage-earners) and its exceptionally high rate of economic growth.[4]

Comparability of national statistics and working time

These global estimates (and the subsequent regional estimates) need to be interpreted with care. First, there are differences across countries in the way wages are estimated by national statistical offices. While the most developed economies carry out regular establishment surveys and specific surveys on the structure of earnings, other countries collect wage data through labour force surveys, and definitions of what is counted as a wage sometimes differ. Coverage can also vary across countries. While the ILO generally seeks to obtain data for all paid employees, in practice coverage is sometimes restricted to certain geographical areas (for example, metropolitan areas) or specific subgroups of employees (for example, non-agricultural employees). As with many other economic variables, these differences make it difficult to compare levels across countries. Yet it is still possible to draw meaningful conclusions about changes over time.

Secondly, changes in monthly average wages summarize innumerable changes at enterprise level and at sectoral level, including not only changes in the hourly wage rate but also changes in the number of hours worked. In many countries the global economic crisis has led to shorter hours of work owing to reductions in the amount of overtime, an increase in time-related underemployment, and/or an increase in the proportion of part-time relative to full-time employees, all of which negatively affect total monthly wages. Various countries have also implemented "work-sharing" programmes: reductions in working time in order to avoid lay-offs.[5] Most typically, a three- or four-day working week has replaced the more usual five-day working week. In other instances, daily hours have been reduced or plants have been temporarily shut down for periods of several weeks or even months. A reduction in working hours usually leads to proportional reductions in monthly wages, but in the context of "work-sharing" programmes governments have often provided wage supplements through partial unemployment compensation.[6]

The "composition effect"

The use of aggregate wage data, as opposed to tracking a panel of individuals, may also give rise to what is known as a "composition effect": a change in average wage levels that results from a change in the composition of the wage-earner segment of the labour force rather than from changes in earnings of those who remain employed throughout. This may introduce a bias. As pointed out in the previous edition of the *Global Wage Report* (ILO, 2010a), this bias may be "countercyclical", meaning that aggregate data may underestimate the decline in the real wages of individuals who keep their jobs during recessions and, later, underestimate the upward trend in their wages during recoveries. For example, low-skilled workers with temporary employment contracts might be the first to be dismissed by enterprises during a recession. Since the remaining workforce then consists of relatively better-paid workers, this can bias trends in average wages upwards. The reverse effect might be observed during the recovery, if low-paid workers are the first to be rehired (see also ILO, 2012b).

2.2 The gender pay gap

A smaller gap but women may not be better off

Figure 4 presents changes in the average gender pay gap between 1999–2007 and 2008–11, illustrating the evolution of the gap in all countries over the crisis where such data are available. As the data show, the gender pay gap has declined in the crisis years in most countries. However, interpretation of this decline is complicated by the "composition effect", as a narrowing of the gender pay gap does not necessarily imply that the situation of women has improved. The case of Estonia shows how a decline in the gender pay gap can be achieved not through improvements in the situation of

Figure 4 The gender pay gap (GPG), 1999–2007 and 2008–11

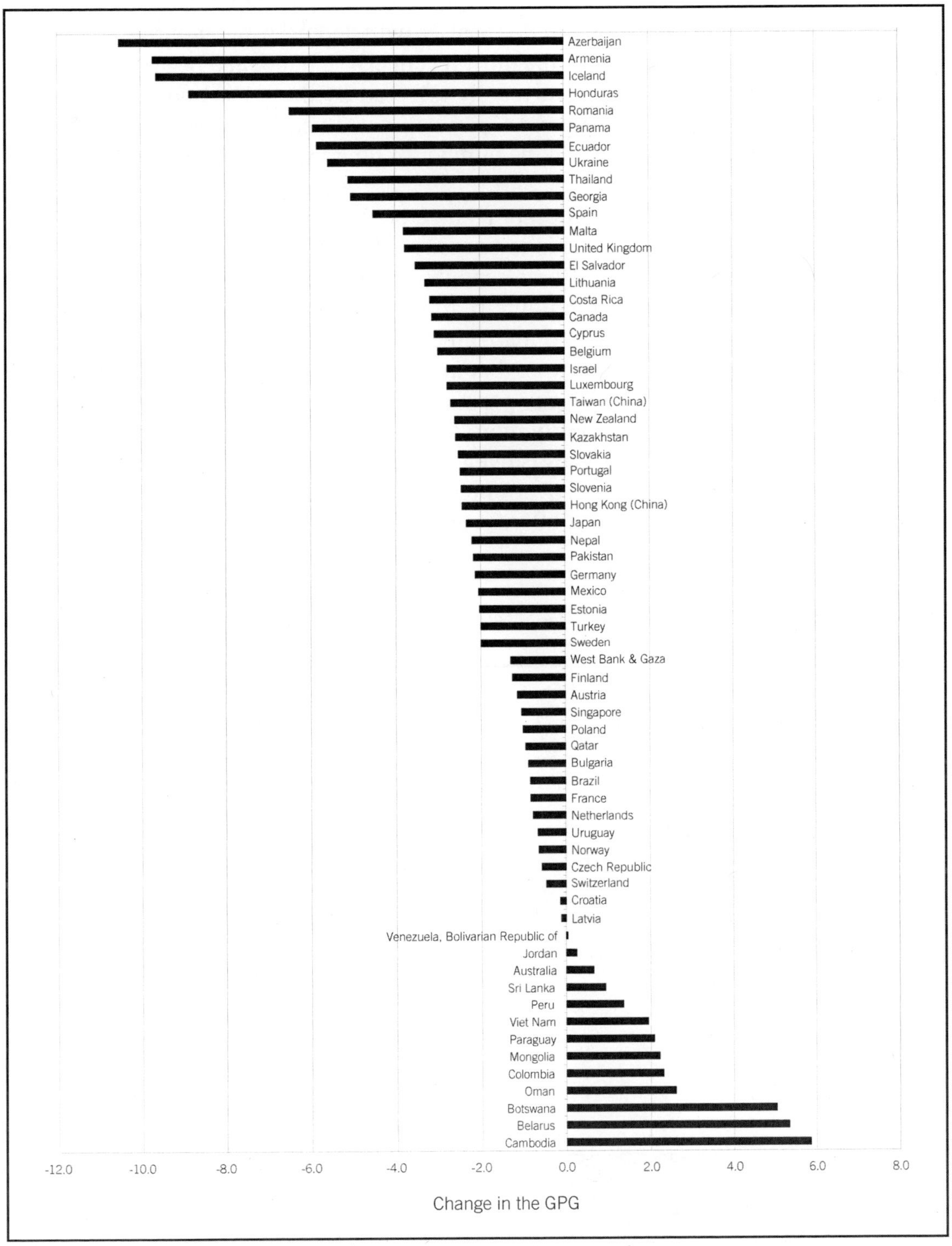

Note: The gender pay gap (GPG) is defined as GPG = ((*Em* – *Ew*)/ *Em*)*100, where *Em* stands for the average wage of men and *Ew* is the average wage of women (see ILO, 2012b). The change in the GPG is defined as the average of the GPG between 2008 and 11 minus the average of the GPG between 1997 and 2007. Data are not available for all countries for all years; averages for the two periods are calculated using the data available for each country during both periods.
Source: ILO Global Wage Database.

women but through a deterioration of the labour market circumstances of men relative to women. Figure 5 illustrates the tendency for the gender pay gap in Estonia to change in a pro-cyclical fashion, widening in times of growth and narrowing during recession. The marked decline in 2009, during the most recent crisis, happened because men were more concentrated in sectors most adversely affected by the crisis and worked fewer hours. Consequently, in 2009 the gender pay gap narrowed because of a decrease in male wages as a result of a decline in the number of hours worked by men (see Anspal, Kraut and Rõõm, 2010.)

Figure 4 focuses on the direction of change between the two periods, rather than on differences among countries. This is because differences in the data sources and/or employee coverage used by different countries affect estimates of the gender pay gap. The case of Norway, shown in figure 6, illustrates how the gender pay gap varies depending on whether all, full-time, or part-time employees are chosen. The gender pay gap for part-time work is low, indicating that men and women who work part-time have similar pay. In contrast, the gender pay gap for full-time employees is higher, as male full-time employees earn considerably more than female full-time employees. Finally, the gender pay gap for all employees is even higher than that for full-time employees, owing to the fact that women are overrepresented among part-time workers, whose hourly wage rates were only about 80 per cent of those of full-time workers in 2011.

Figure 5 The gender pay gap in Estonia, 1993–2009

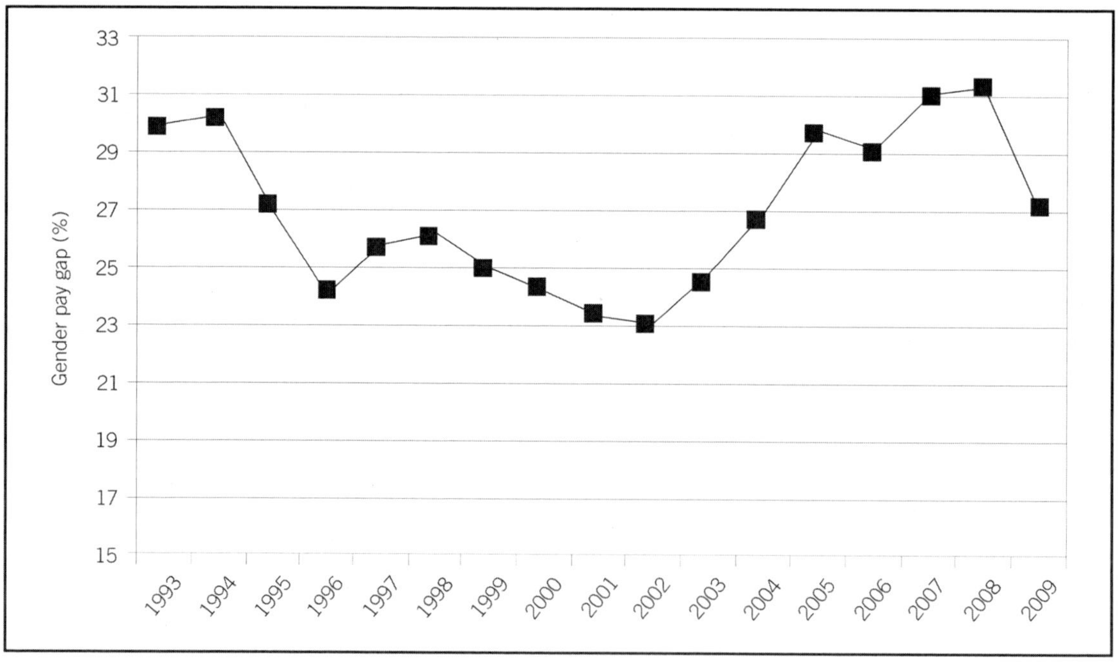

Note: The gender pay gap (GPG) is defined as GPG = ((*Em* – *Ew*)/ *Em*)*100, where *Em* stands for the average wage of men and *Ew* is the average wage of women (see ILO, 2012b).

Source: Graph reproduced from Anspal, Kraut and Rõõm, 2010.

Figure 6 The gender pay gap in Norway by employment status, 2008–11

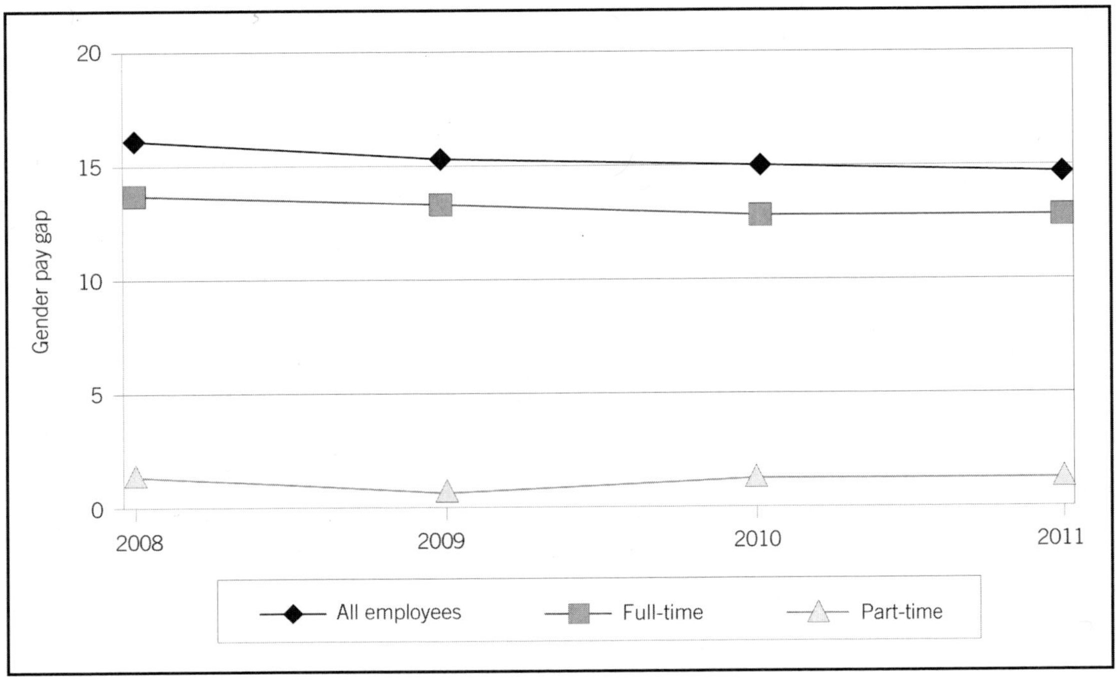

Note: The gender pay gap (GPG) is defined as GPG = ((*Em* – *Ew*)/ *Em*)*100, where *Em* stands for the average wage of men and *Ew* is the average wage of women (see ILO, 2012b).
Source: ILO calculations based on data from Statistics Norway.

Changes over time are less sensitive to employee coverage. Even so, interpretation of changes in the gender pay gap over time should be considered alongside other labour market indicators which reflect changes in the conditions of work and employment for women.

3 Regional estimates

3.1 Overall growth masks a complex picture

As noted above, there are large differences in the growth rate of real average wages across regions and countries, with wages generally growing faster in areas of stronger economic growth. Figure 7 shows our estimates of the growth of real monthly average wages by region from 2006, including the years of the crisis. As with our global estimate, the regional estimates are weighted estimates (as explained in Appendix I) and so are heavily influenced by wage trends in larger economies, such as China in Asia, the United States in the developed economies, Russia and Ukraine in Eastern Europe and Central Asia, Brazil or Mexico in Latin America and the Caribbean, or South Africa in the

Figure 7 Annual average real wage growth by region, 2006–11

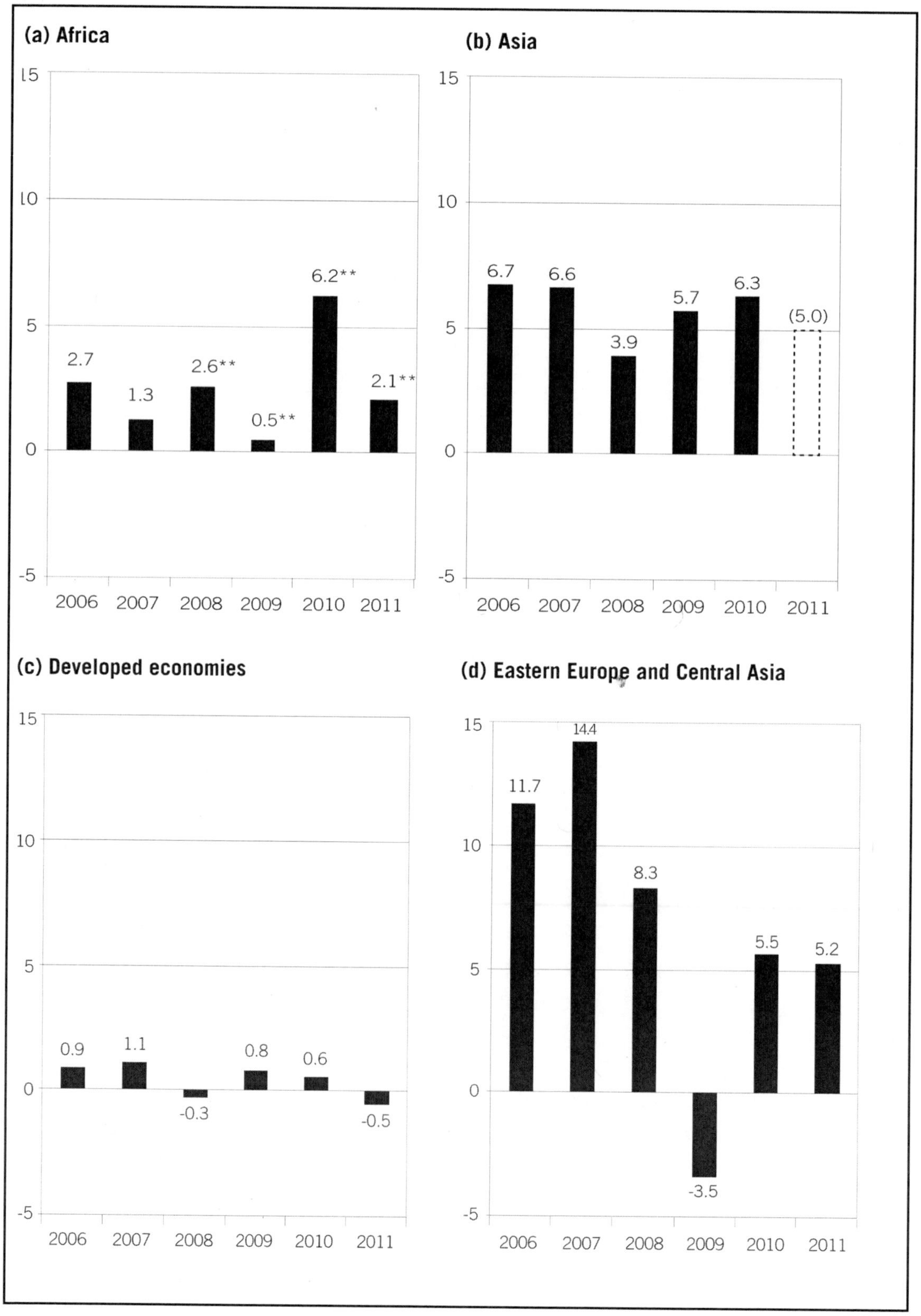

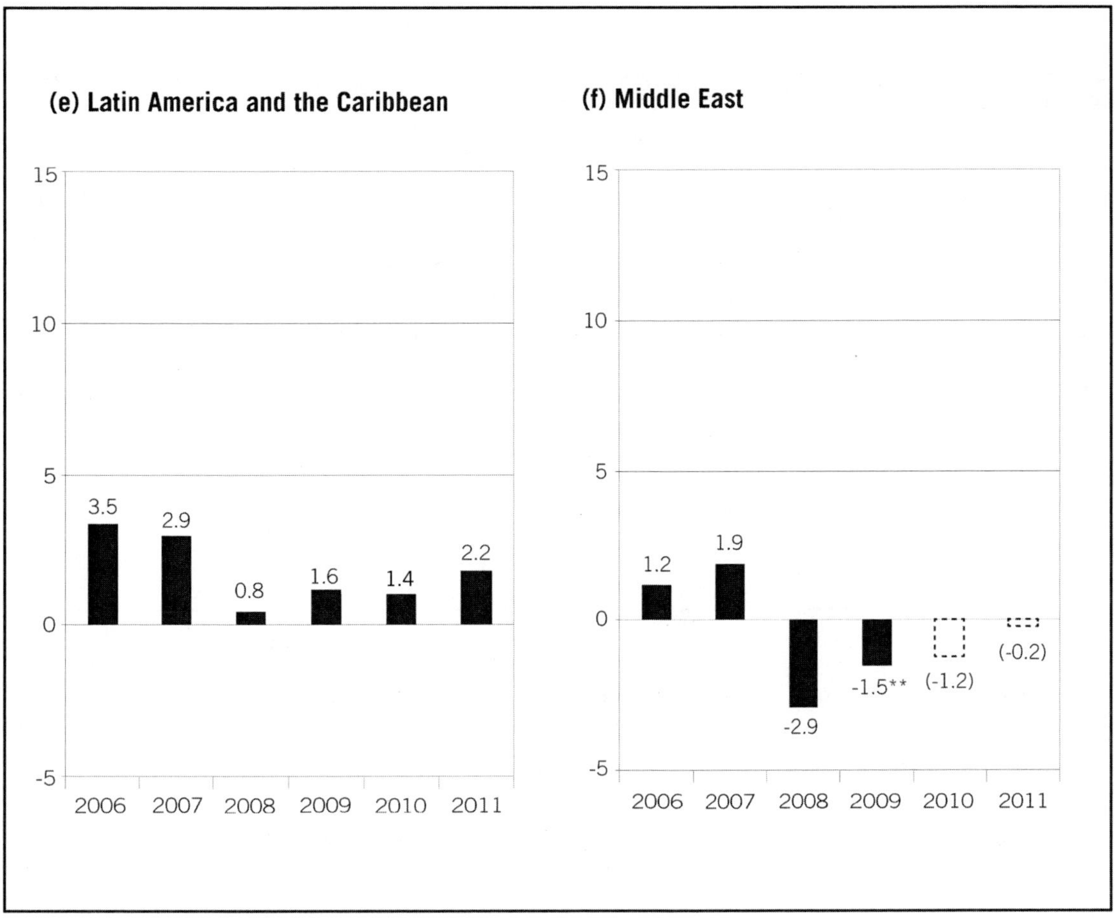

* Growth rates published as "provisional estimates" (based on coverage of c.75 %).
** Growth rates published as "tentative estimates" (based on coverage of c.40–c.74%).
() Growth rates published but likely to change (based on coverage of less than 40%).
Note: For coverage and methodology, see Appendix I.
Source: ILO Global Wage Database.

African continent. We see that in developed economies the growth of real wages fluctuated within a narrow range of approximately plus and minus 1 per cent. In other regions, the fluctuations were typically larger.

Table 1 takes a longer view and shows the cumulative increase in real average wages since 2000. We see that between 2000 and 2011 global real monthly average wages increased by close to one quarter, but differences across regions are stark. In Asia real average wages approximately doubled, in Latin America and the Caribbean as well as in Africa they increased by slightly less than the world average, while in developed economies they increased by about 5 per cent. In Eastern Europe and Central Asia average wages almost tripled: as will be shown later, this was in part a recovery of the ground that was lost in the early phase of the transition towards market economies in the 1990s. In the Middle East, our tentative estimates suggest that wages may have declined.

Table 1 Cumulative real wage growth by region since 2000 (index: 2000 = 100)

Regional group	2000	2006	2007	2008	2009	2010	2011
Africa	100.0	103.9	105.3	108.1**	108.6**	115.4**	117.8**
Asia	100.0	149.0	158.8	165.1	174.6	185.6	(194.9)
Eastern Europe and Central Asia	100.0	204.4	233.9	253.4	244.4	257.9	271.3
Developed economies	100.0	103.3	104.5	104.1	104.9	105.5	105.0
Latin America and the Caribbean	100.0	105.4	108.5	109.3	111.0	112.6	115.1
Middle East	100.0	98.3	100.1	97.2	95.8**	(94.6)	(94.4)
World	100.0	112.8	116.1	117.3	118.8	121.3	122.7*

* Growth rates published as "Provisional estimates" (based on coverage of *c.* 75%).
** Growth rates published as "Tentative estimates" (based on coverage of *c.* 40%– *c.* 74%).
() Growth rates published but likely to change (based on coverage of less than 40%).
Note: For coverage and methodology, see Appendix I.
Source: ILO Global Wage Database.

In spite of the faster growth in real average wages in emerging regions over the last decade, absolute differences in wage levels across countries and regions remain considerable. Figure 8 shows estimates by the US Bureau of Labor Statistics comparing hourly direct pay for time worked in manufacturing in 2010. The hourly rate of pay varied from almost US$35 in Denmark, through a little more than US$23 in the United States, to US$13 in Greece, between US$5 and US$6 in Brazil, and less than US$1.50 in the Philippines. Using a different and non-comparable methodology, total hourly compensation costs in manufacturing were estimated at US$1.36 in China for 2008 and at US$1.17 in India for 2007 (United States Department of Labor, Bureau of Labor Statistics, 2011). Although these differences are measured in current US dollars and therefore are dependent on exchange rate fluctuations, they nonetheless point towards the persistence of wide gaps in wages and labour productivity across the world.

3.2 Developed economies

Wages and inflation

In developed economies, average wages underwent a double dip, falling in 2008 and again in 2011 (see figure 7).[7] Figure 9, which highlights trends in *nominal* average wages and price inflation in advanced economies, shows that in 2008 unusually high inflation exceeded nominal wage increases, and hence led to falling real wages.[8] In 2009, the year of the global economic recession, both nominal wages and consumer prices more or less froze. Since then, the recovery of nominal wage growth stalled in 2011 but the increase in consumer prices returned to pre-crisis rates, which explains the fall in real wages in that year.

Figure 8 International comparison of hourly direct pay for time worked in manufacturing, 2010 (US$)

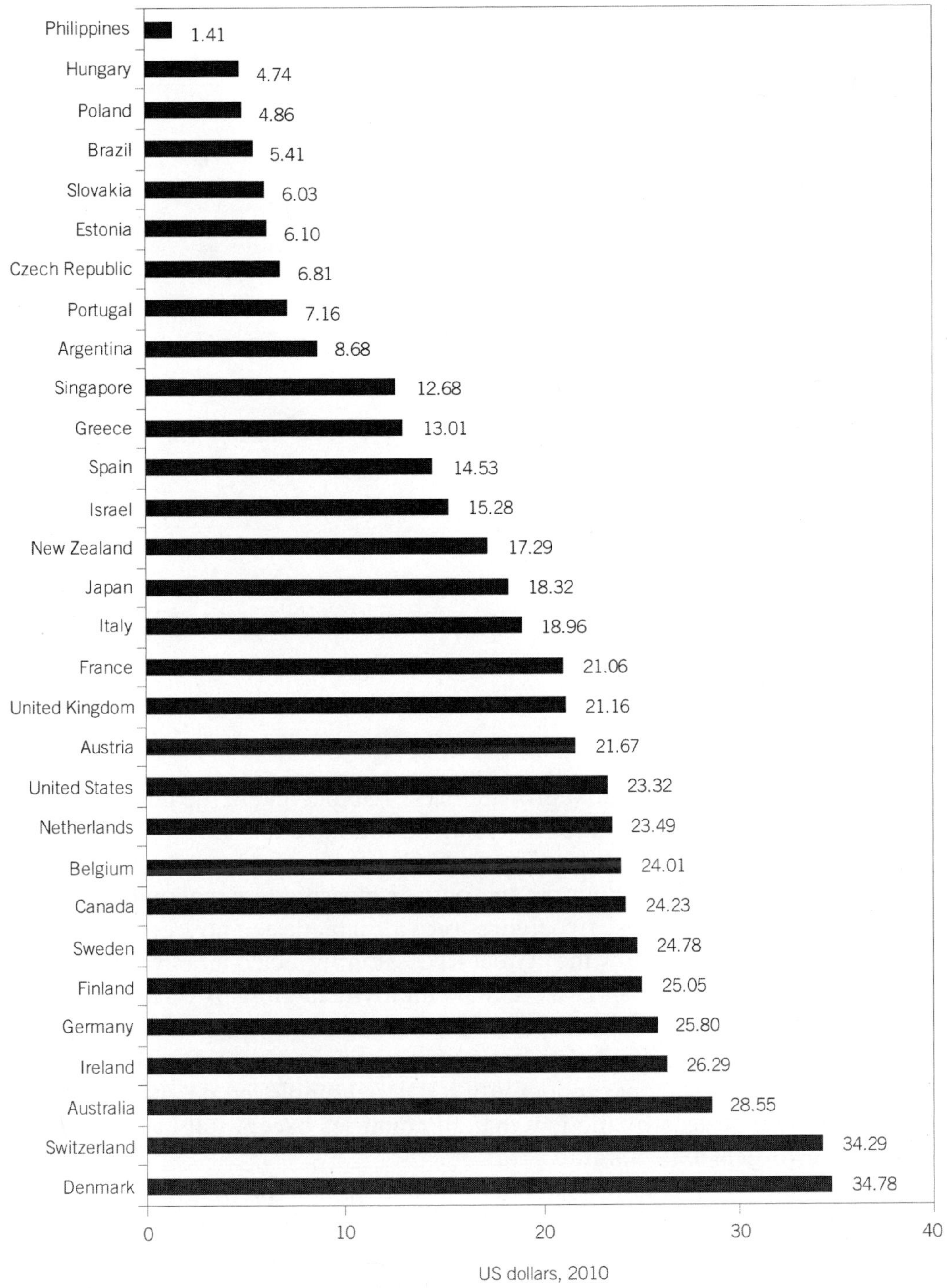

Note: Direct pay for time worked is wages and salaries for time actually worked.

Source: United States Department of Labor, Bureau of Labor Statistics (BLS), 2011.

Figure 9 Trends in nominal wage growth and inflation in advanced economies, 2006–11 (%)

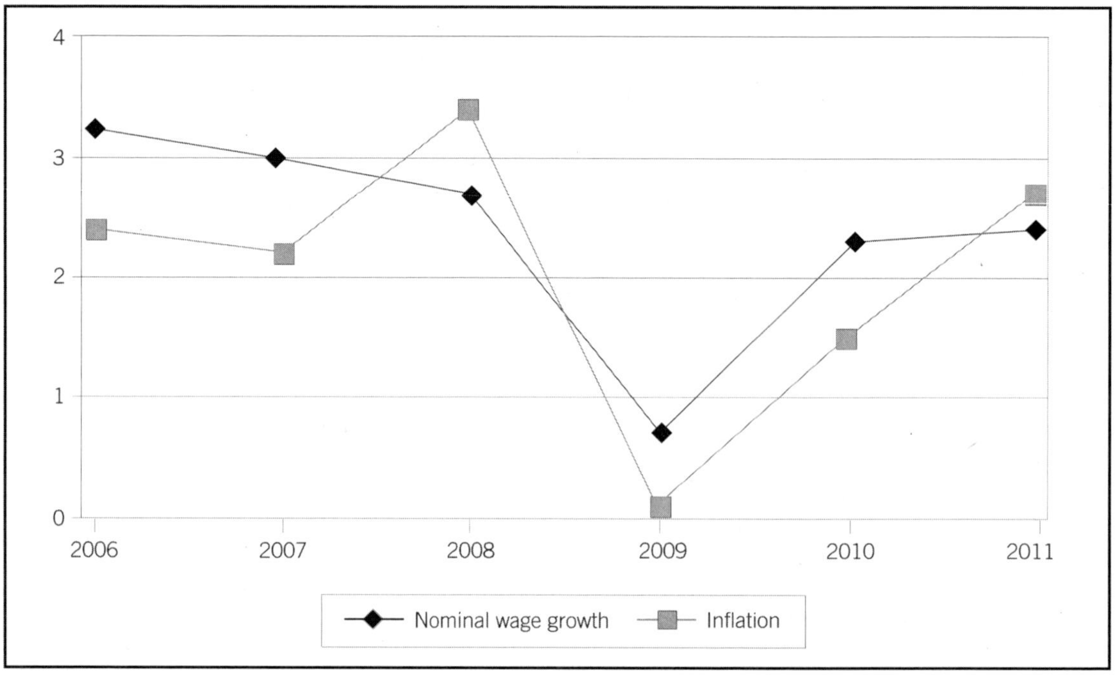

Note: The figure exclusively refers to countries classified by the IMF *World Economic Outlook* report as "advanced economies" and hence excludes certain countries classified in this report as "developed economies" (for a list of these countries, see Appendix I). Nominal wage growth and inflation figures are not strictly comparable across countries owing to differences in the way each country is weighted in the regional estimate. The figure nonetheless illustrates the argument in the text.
Sources: ILO Global WageDatabase; IMF World Economic Outlook database.

Wages and productivity

Figure 10 shows the average annual growth rates in output and in the number of people employed in developed countries for the years before the crisis (1999–2007) and after the beginning of the crisis (2008–11). Figure 11 shows the average annual growth rates of real average wages and of labour productivity as measured by real output per person employed.[9] Taken together, these two figures provide a picture of how economic growth affected the labour force and how the "Great Recession" affected labour markets. Looking at the period before the crisis, we see that employment grew by an amount equal to or less than GDP in almost all countries (as can be seen by the fact that only Italy and Spain lie to the right of the 45-degree line bisecting figure 10(a)). Because GDP grew faster than employment, labour productivity (GDP per employed person) by definition increased. This can be seen by the fact that all countries except Italy and Spain lie on the right of the vertical axis in figure 11(a).

Did the growth of labour productivity translate into higher real wages? Figure 11 shows that most countries did indeed experience a period of growth in both real wages and productivity (indicated by the cluster of countries in the top right corner of figure 11(a)). In a number of countries, such as in Denmark, France, Finland, the United Kingdom, Romania and the Czech Republic, there was a close connection between wage and productivity growth (as shown in figure 11). But there are also many countries where the two variables were less closely synchronized. Figure 11(a) shows

Figure 10 Growth in output and employment in developed economies, 1999–2007 and 2008–11 (%)

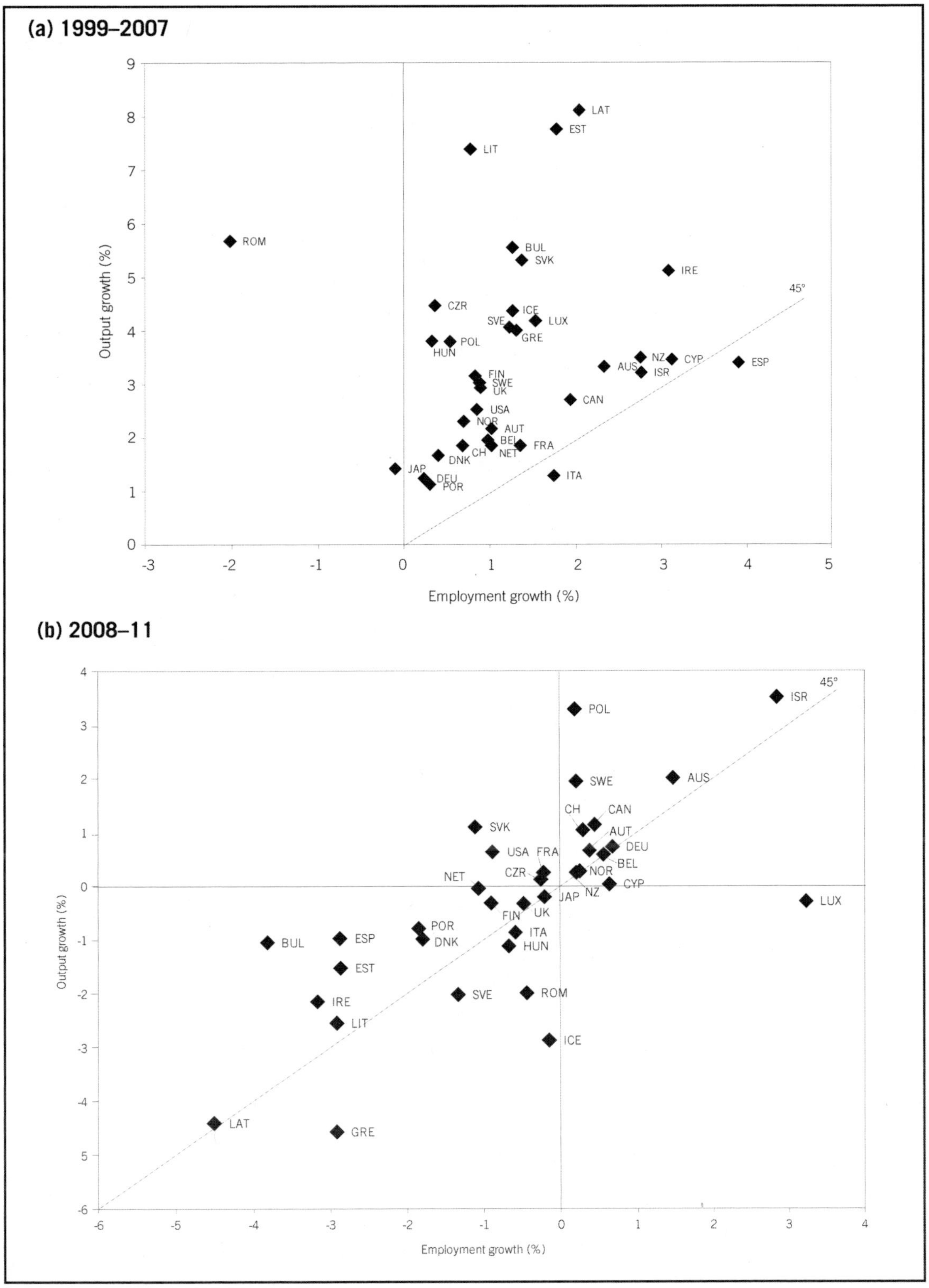

Note: For country abbreviations, see Appendix I.

Sources: ILO Trends Econometric Model, March 2012; IMF World Economic Outlook database.

Figure 11 Growth in real wages and labour productivity in developed economies, 1999–2007 and 2008–11 (%)

(a) 1999–2007

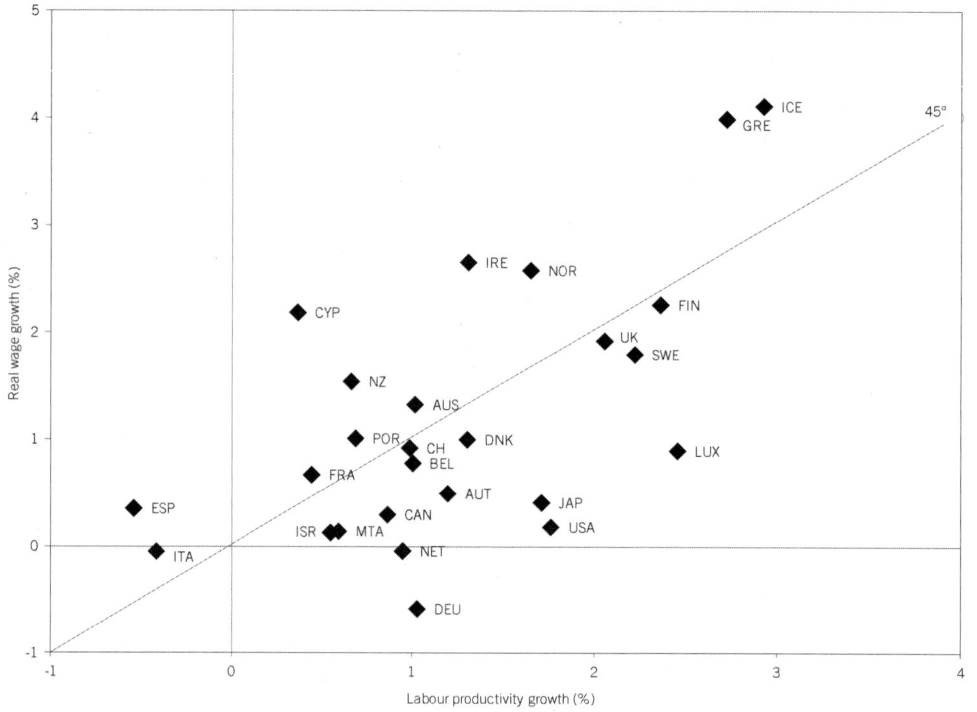

(b) 2008–11

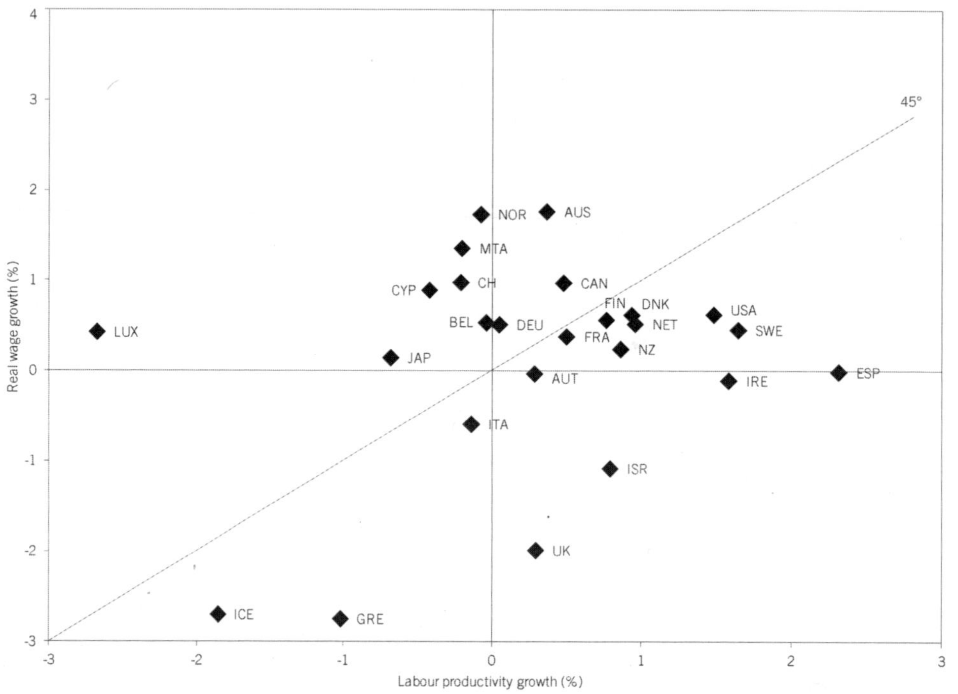

(c) 1999–2007

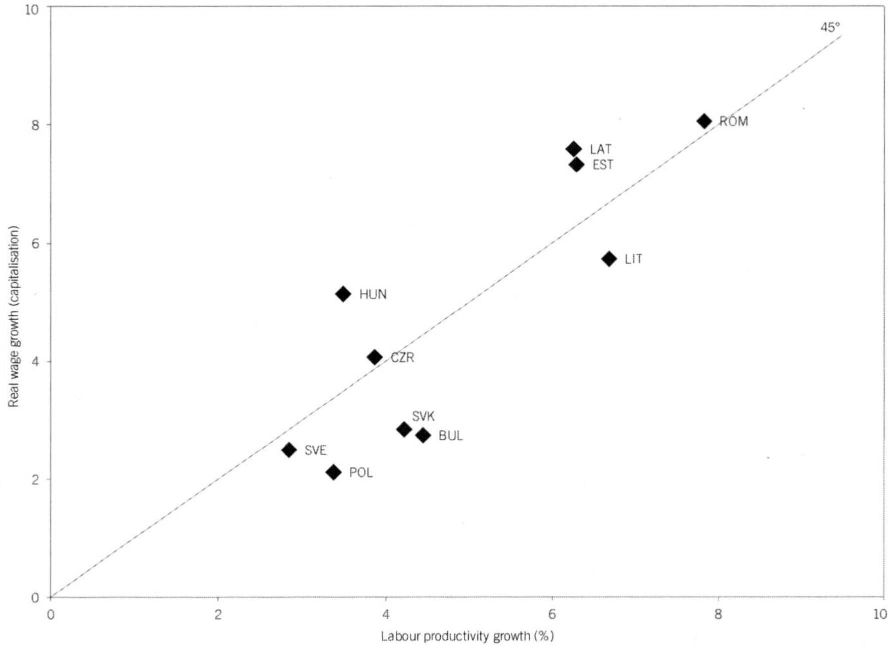

(d) 2008–11

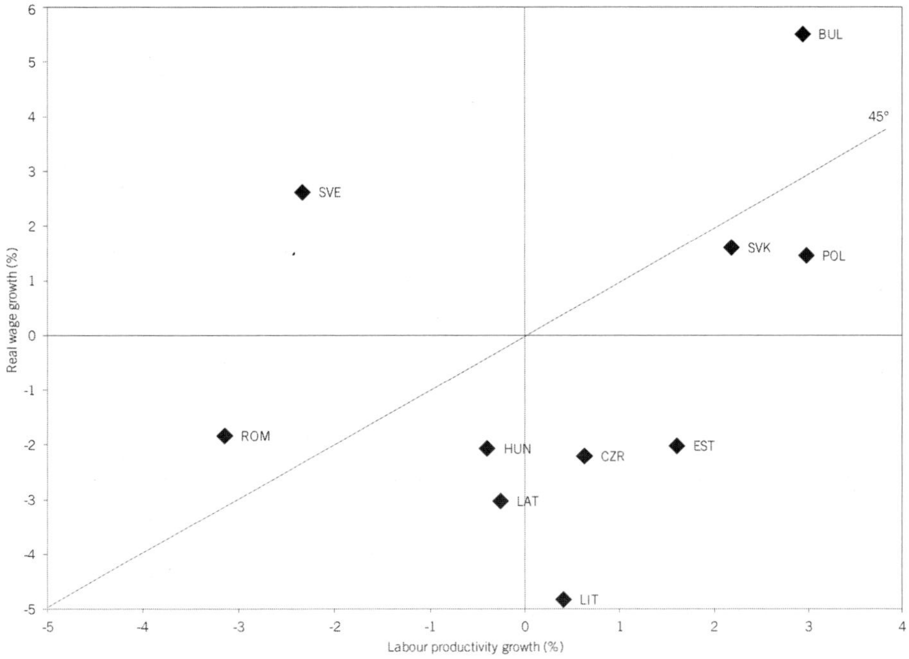

Note: Both the top (a–b) and bottom (c–d) pairs of graphs refer to countries in the developed economies region. They have been separated only for reasons of legibility. If 1999, 2007, 2008 or 2011 data were unavailable, the next closest period's data point was used to estimate the trend. For country abbreviations, see Appendix I.

Sources: ILO Global Wage Database; ILO Trends Econometric Model, March 2012.

that in Greece and Iceland average wages grew ahead of labour productivity, while in Spain and Italy labour productivity declined but wages did so only marginally (in the case of Italy) or not at all (in the case of Spain). In some of the largest economies of the region, by contrast, wage growth trailed behind productivity growth: this occurred in the United States, in Japan and especially in Germany, where average wages declined in spite of positive average labour productivity growth in the years 1999–2007 (see figure 35 for more details on Germany).

Economic growth and employment growth

What has happened in the years since the "Great Recession"? It is apparent from figure 10(b) that all those countries where GDP contracted on average over 2008–11 also saw employment falling or at best static (with the exception of Luxembourg, where employment grew). Conversely, most economies with positive GDP growth during the crisis also succeeded in expanding employment. Interestingly, though, during the years of the crisis employment suffered more than output in a number of countries, including Spain, Ireland, Portugal and Bulgaria. In the United States, employment fell in spite of slow but positive economic growth.

Consequently, it is clear from figures 11 (b) and (d), though, that most countries recorded positive labour productivity growth during 2008–11 in spite of the crisis (as shown by the fact that most countries are on the right side of the vertical axis in these sections of the figure). Many of these countries also saw moderate increases in real wages, including Germany, which seems to have changed course of action, allowing for wage growth in excess of labour productivity after years of wage moderation. One of the exceptions is the United Kingdom, where in spite of productivity gains real average wages declined sharply under the influence of relatively high inflation. In some countries wages declined considerably more than labour productivity: these included Greece and some newer EU countries. In Greece, where wages were growing ahead of productivity before the crisis, average wages were forced down by austerity programmes and cumulatively fell by close to 15 per cent over 2010 and 2011 alone. Overall, a comparison of figures 10 and 11 produces little evidence of a simple trade-off between wage moderation and employment growth during the crisis.

3.3 Eastern Europe and Central Asia

From recovery to crisis

In the group of (non-EU) Eastern European and Central Asian countries, the regional growth rate in real average wages fluctuated widely, from double-digit rates before the crisis to the hard landing of 2009. Although positive wage growth returned in 2010 and 2011, the rates reached then were not nearly as high as before the crisis. Taken together, figures 12 and 13 show that before the crisis, output expanded faster than employment (figure 12), as a result of which labour productivity grew in all countries (figure 13). Strikingly, the gains in productivity before the crisis were accompanied by even larger real wage increases of more than 10 per cent a year, on average, in a majority of countries. In many cases, this was a result of the process of recovery from the transition to market economies. Figure 14 shows that real wages in Russia initially fell to less than

Figure 12 Growth in output and employment in Eastern Europe and Central Asia, 1999–2007 and 2008–11 (%)

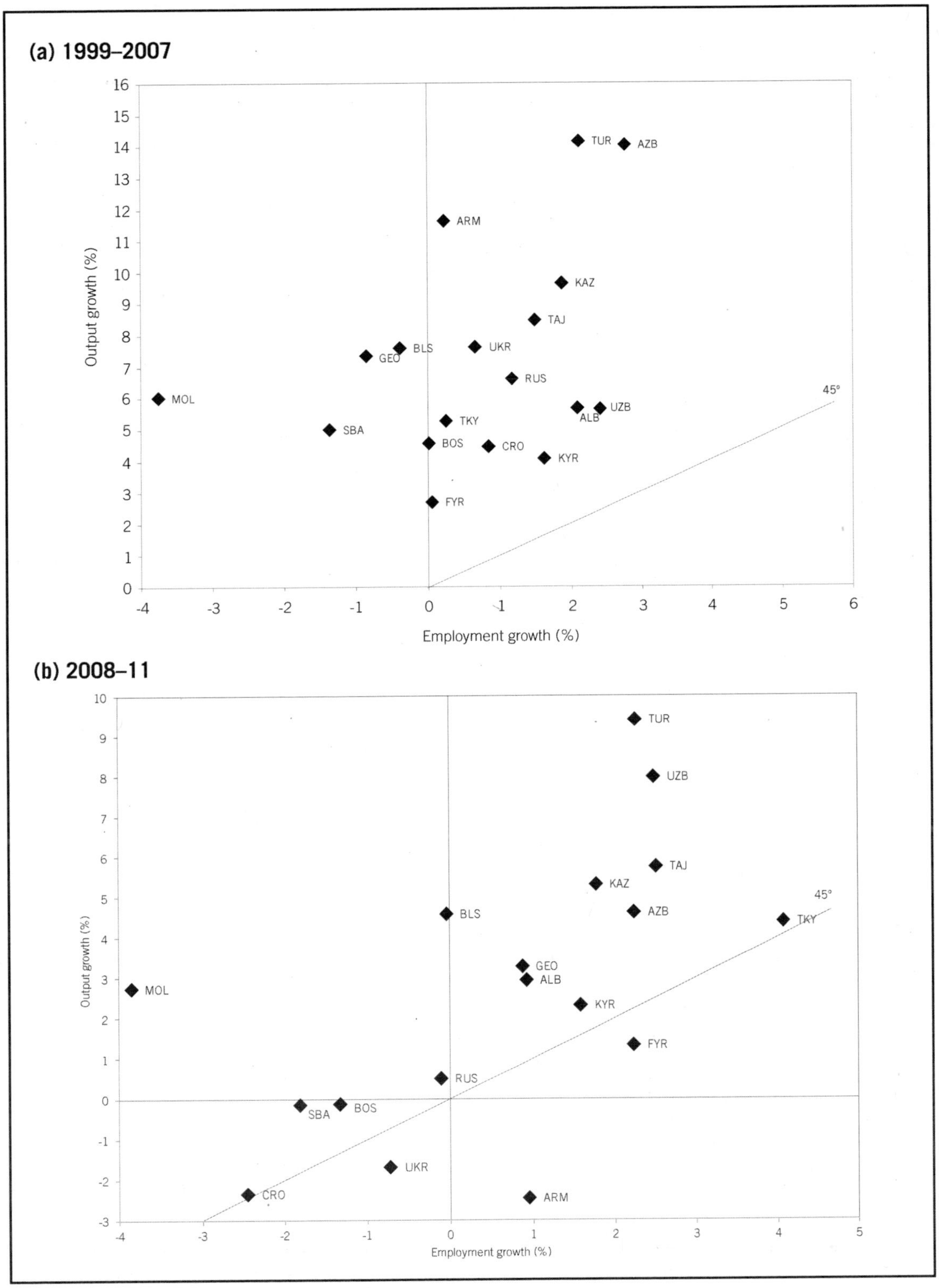

Note: For country abbreviations, see Appendix I.

Sources: ILO Trends Econometric Model, March 2012; IMF World Economic Outlook database.

Figure 13 Growth in wages and labour productivity in Eastern Europe and Central Asia, 1999–2007 and 2008–11 (%)

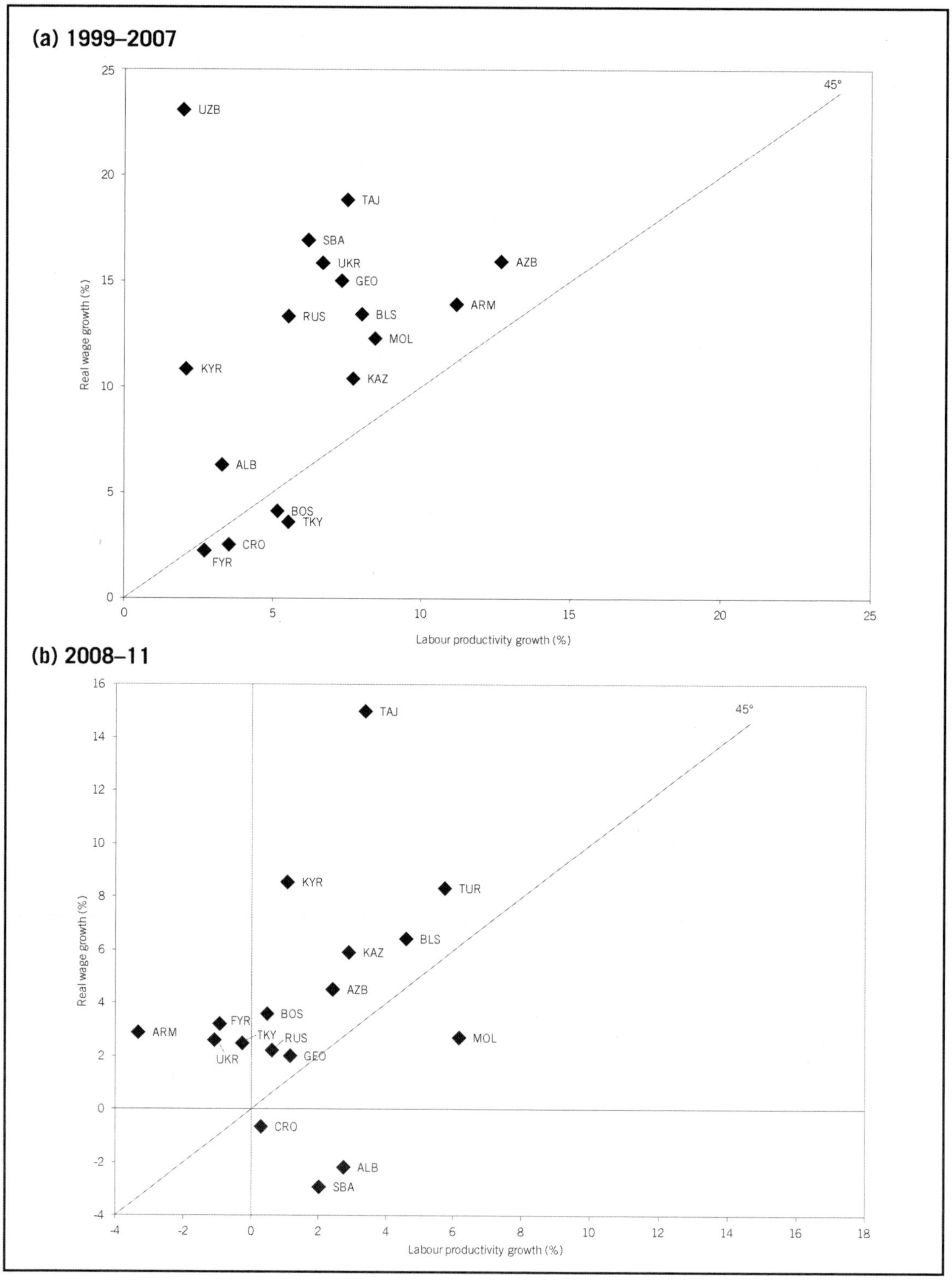

Note: If data for 1999, 2007, 2008 or 2011 were unavailable, the next closest year's data point was used to estimate the trend. For country abbreviations, see Appendix I.

Sources: ILO Global Wage Database; ILO Trends Econometric Model, March 2012.

Figure 14 Index of real wages in the Russian Federation since 1990 (1990 = 100)

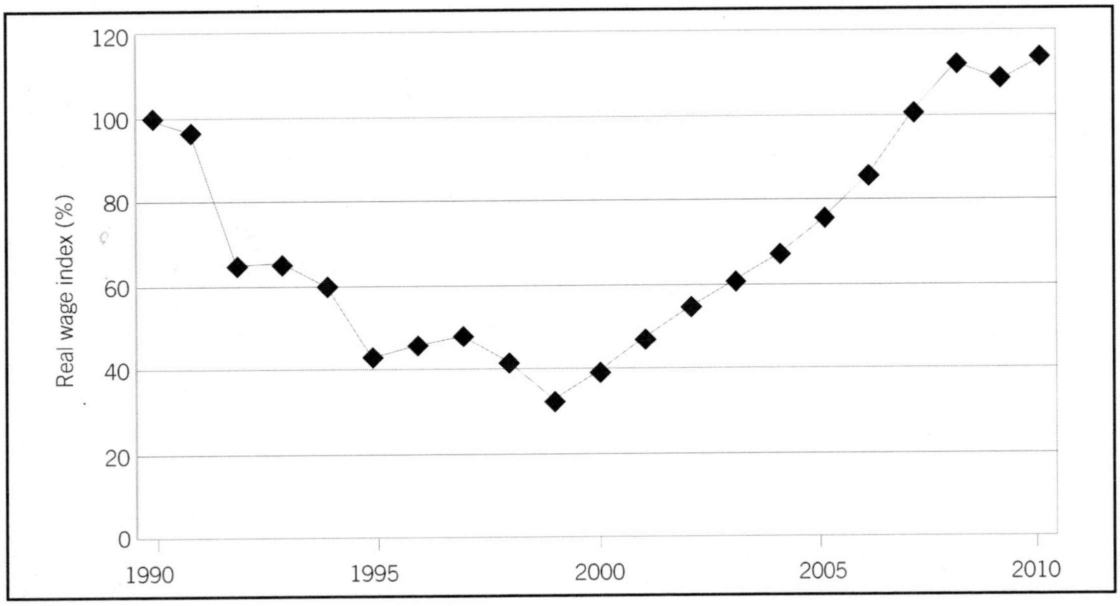

Source: ILO calculations based on data from the Russian Federation Federal State Statistics Service, 2011.

half of their 1990 value, before progressively recovering and tripling in the years after 2000. Ukraine followed a similar pattern, with real wages falling sharply between 1992 and 1999 before increasing more than threefold in real terms up to 2009.[10]

Wages reined in

More recently, between 2008 and 2011, productivity grew more slowly but remained largely positive, and real wage growth became more closely aligned with productivity growth. There were exceptions: in Serbia and Albania, real wages fell in spite of positive labour productivity growth, a reflection of the freezing of nominal wages in the public sector. In Serbia, an agreement with the IMF signed in April 2009 included a commitment by the Serbian Government to keep public sector wages and pensions frozen in nominal terms in 2009 and 2010 – as a result of which real wages in the public administration declined (Arandarenko and Avlijas, 2011). This measure came with a ban on new employment in the public sector. Similarly, on the advice of the IMF, budgetary restrictions on wage growth in the public sector have been introduced in Albania.

But the regional picture shown in figure 7 is most strongly influenced by the trends in the two largest economies, namely the Russian Federation and Ukraine. In both countries wage growth slowed in 2008 and turned negative in 2009, before bouncing back to about half of pre-crisis rates in subsequent years. An analysis of the impact of the crisis on the Ukrainian labour market reveals that much of the decline in monthly wages was due to an increase in involuntary underemployment in 2009, when every fifth employee in Ukraine worked fewer hours than he or she would have liked. Many employees had to go on unpaid leave, especially in the industrial sector (ILO, 2011d),[11] while others saw their basic wages frozen and their bonuses cut (Kulikov and Blyzniuk, 2010).

3.4 Asia and the Pacific

High growth, dominated by China

The trends in Asia, and particularly in East Asia, contrast sharply with those in other regions. Reflecting the region's resilient economic performance during the crisis, wages in Asia have continued to grow at high rates (as shown in figure 7). This particularly reflects the influence of China, where wages in "urban units" increased on average at double-digit annual rates over the full decade, according to the *China Yearbook of Statistics*. Using these official figures of an annual rate of growth of 12 per cent per annum, real average wages in China have more than tripled over the decade from 2000 to 2010, prompting questions about the possible end of "cheap labour" in China. In figure 15, we see that without China, where the growth of GDP and wages was exceptionally high during the past years, the picture looks considerably different, reflecting the less positive story of wages in countries such as the Republic of Korea or India during the last four years.

Looking at figures 16 and 17, we see that most countries in the region had economic growth rates that averaged 5 per cent or more in the years 1999–2007, accompanied in the sub-period from 2002 to 2007 by average annual employment growth of 1.2 per cent in East Asia, 1.8 per cent per annum in South-East Asia and the Pacific, and 2.2 per cent in South Asia (ILO, 2012a). It must be emphasized at this point, however, that the growth in overall employment in developing countries – where most people cannot afford to be unemployed – is closely related to trends in

Figure 15 Annual average real wage growth in Asia, 2006–11

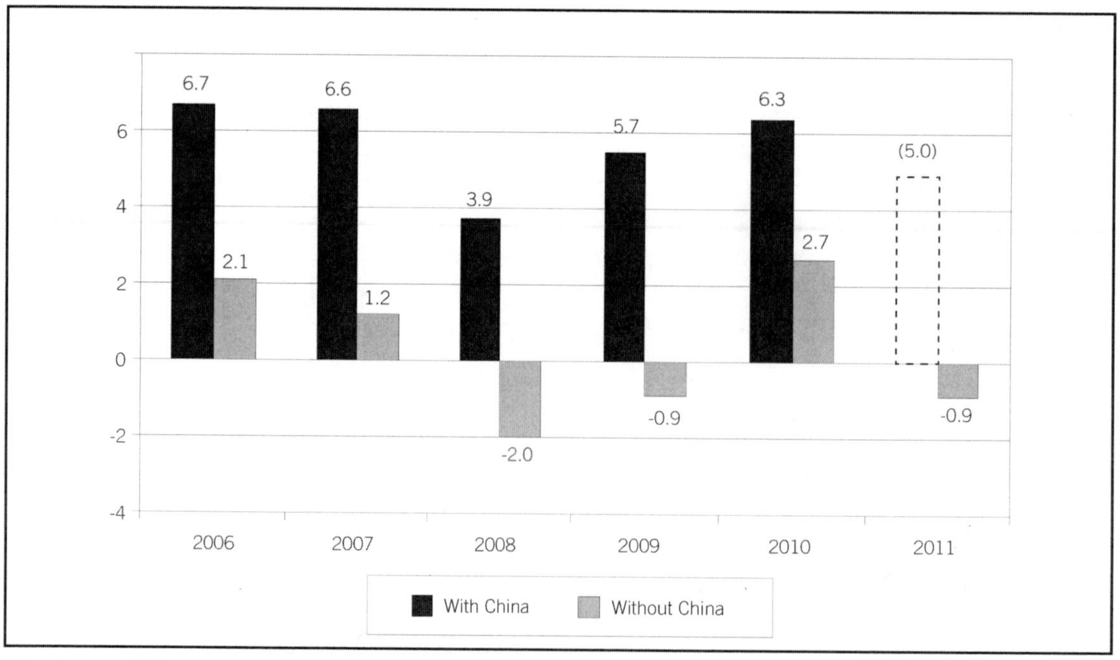

() Growth rates published but likely to change (based on coverage of less than 40%).

Note: For coverage and methodology, see Appendix I.

Source: ILO Global Wage Database.

Figure 16 Growth in output and employment in Asia, 1997–2007 and 2008–11 (%)

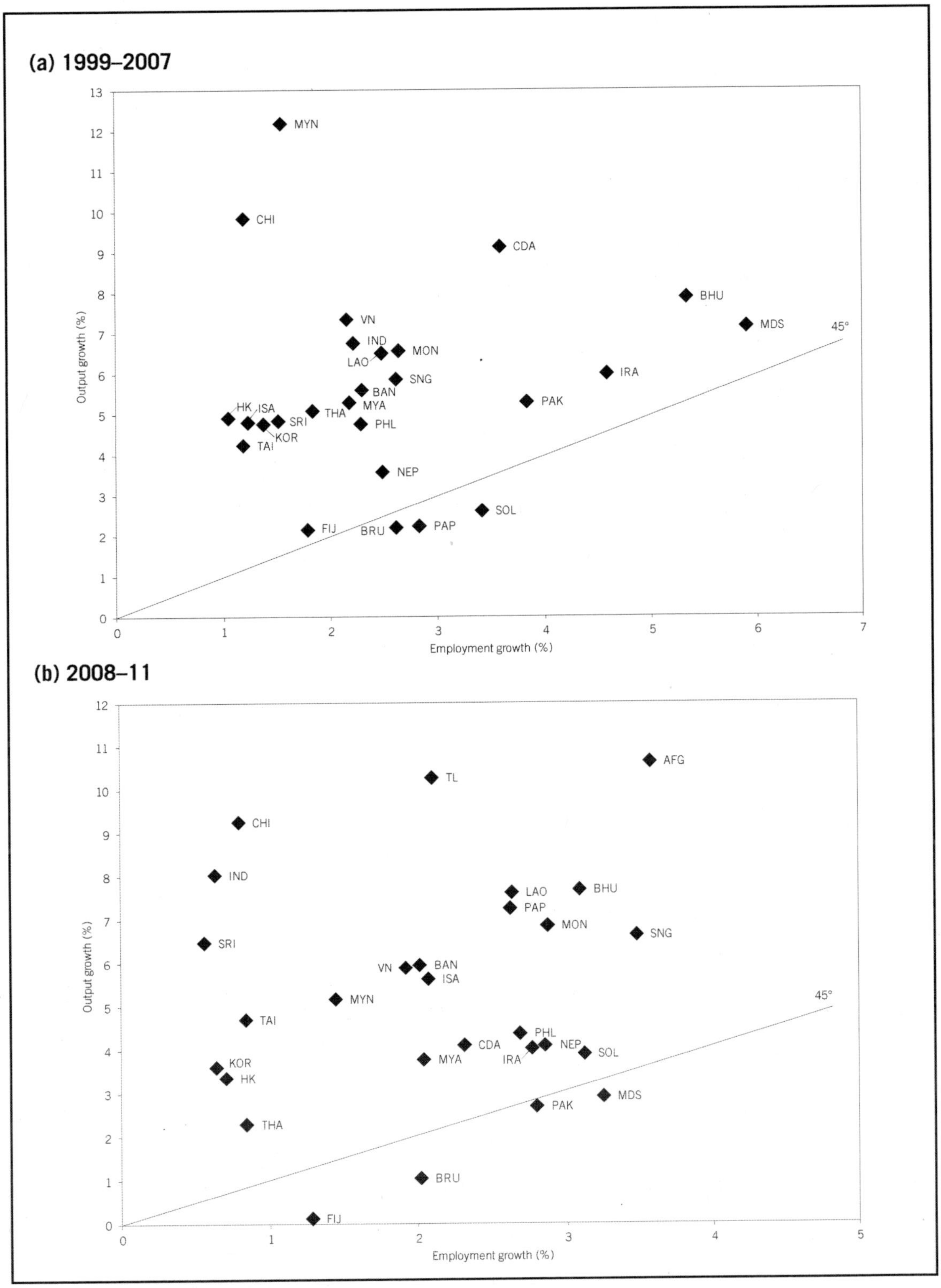

Note: For country abbreviations, see Appendix I.

Sources: ILO Trends Econometric Model, March 2012; IMF World Economic Outlook database.

Figure 17 Growth in output and in numbers of paid employees in Asia, 1997–2007 and 2008–11 (%)

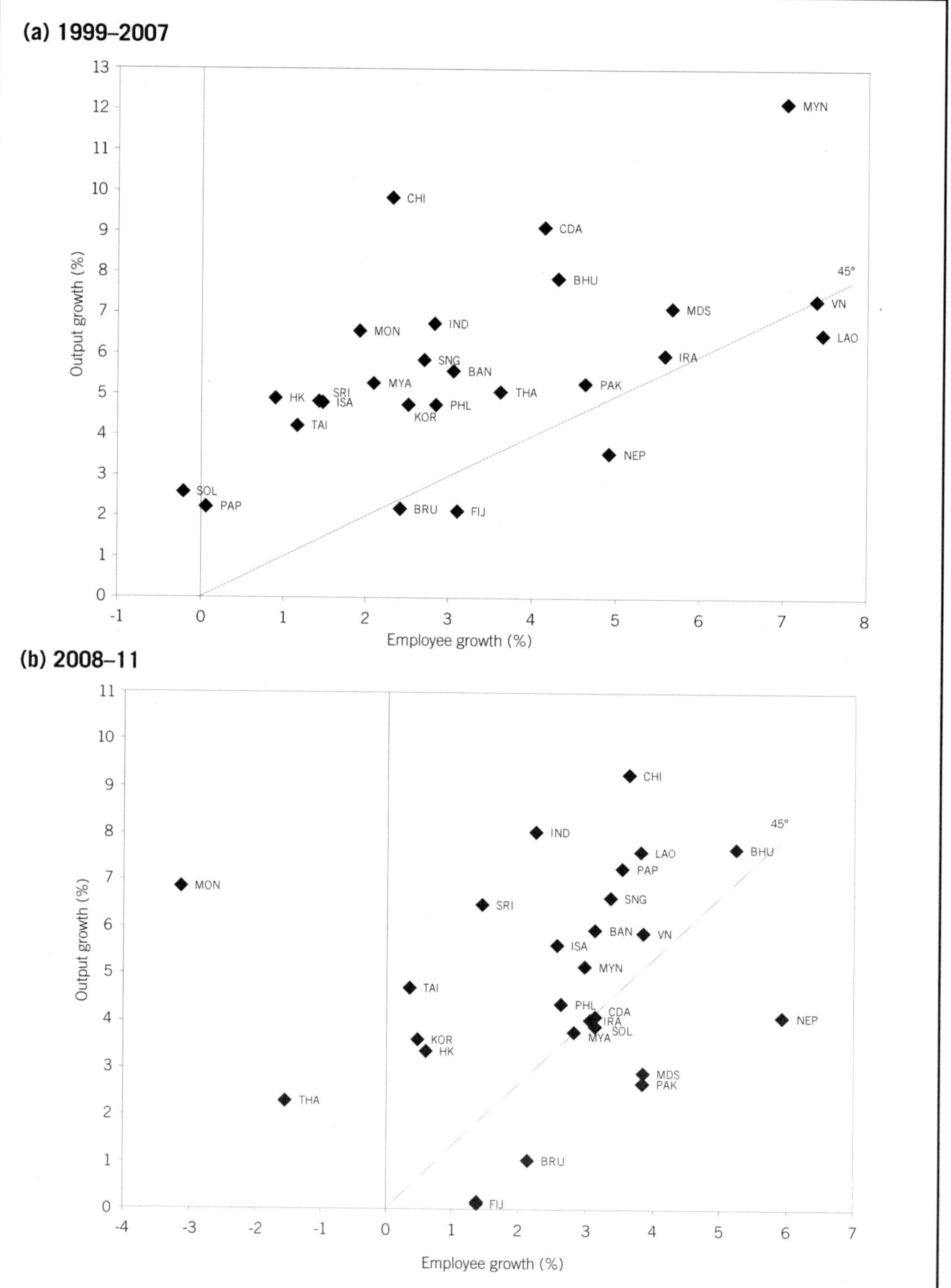

Note: For country abbreviations, see Appendix I.

Sources: ILO Trends Econometric Model, March 2012; IMF World Economic Outlook database.

the size of the labour force. Hence we also present GDP growth alongside the growth in the number of paid employees in figure 17, which leaves out the self-employed or family helpers. Even so, we see that output growth exceeded the growth of paid employment in most countries.

A caveat on labour productivity: the role of paid employment

What has been the impact on wages of these growth rates? The juxtaposition of data on average wage growth and labour productivity, as in figure 18, must be interpreted with care in developing countries. This is because average wages refer to the earnings of *paid* employees (who represent less than 50 per cent of workers in some Asian countries), while labour productivity measures the GDP of *all* employed people (both employees and self-employed). A better comparison would be between average wages and the productivity of paid employees, but data on the latter are generally not available. In principle, one suspects that the growth in output across all workers underestimates the growth in labour productivity of paid employees, a substantial proportion of whom work in the more productive and dynamic industrial sectors. Also, when comparing wage growth and productivity growth in China, one must keep in mind that the former only cover State-owned enterprises, collective-owned units and other type of companies linked to the State (see note 4). The decline in the labour share in China documented in Part II of this report suggests that wage growth was in fact lower than productivity growth in China.

Purchasing power under threat

In spite of these caveats, figure 18 clearly shows that in general gains in both productivity and real wages have been positive, and quite substantial, both before and during the years of the crisis. Yet in some countries, wage growth as measured by official statistics was clearly disappointing over the period 1999–2007. Among the East Asian countries, relatively low wage growth was recorded, for example, in Thailand. In South Asia, too, measures of real average wages stagnated in the decade before the crisis. In India, wage trends are somewhat unclear. The authoritative sources of data on wage growth in India are the Annual Survey of Industries by the Central Statistics Office and the real wage index published by the Labour Bureau. Both data sources indicate that real wages declined in a majority of recent years, shrinking the purchasing power of wage earners. This would explain the many concerns expressed by workers in India about rapidly increasing prices, particularly food prices. The trend, however, is surprising in the light of the country's rapid economic growth over the last decade. It also contrasts with our analysis of the Employment–Unemployment Survey from the National Sample Survey Office (NSSO), conducted every five years along with the Consumer Expenditure Survey, in which salaried and casual workers report a 150 per cent increase in their earnings – much higher than the 52 per cent increase in the consumer price index – in the five years between 2004/05 and 2009/10.

Figure 18 Growth in wages and labour productivity in Asia, 1997–2007 and 2008–11 (%)

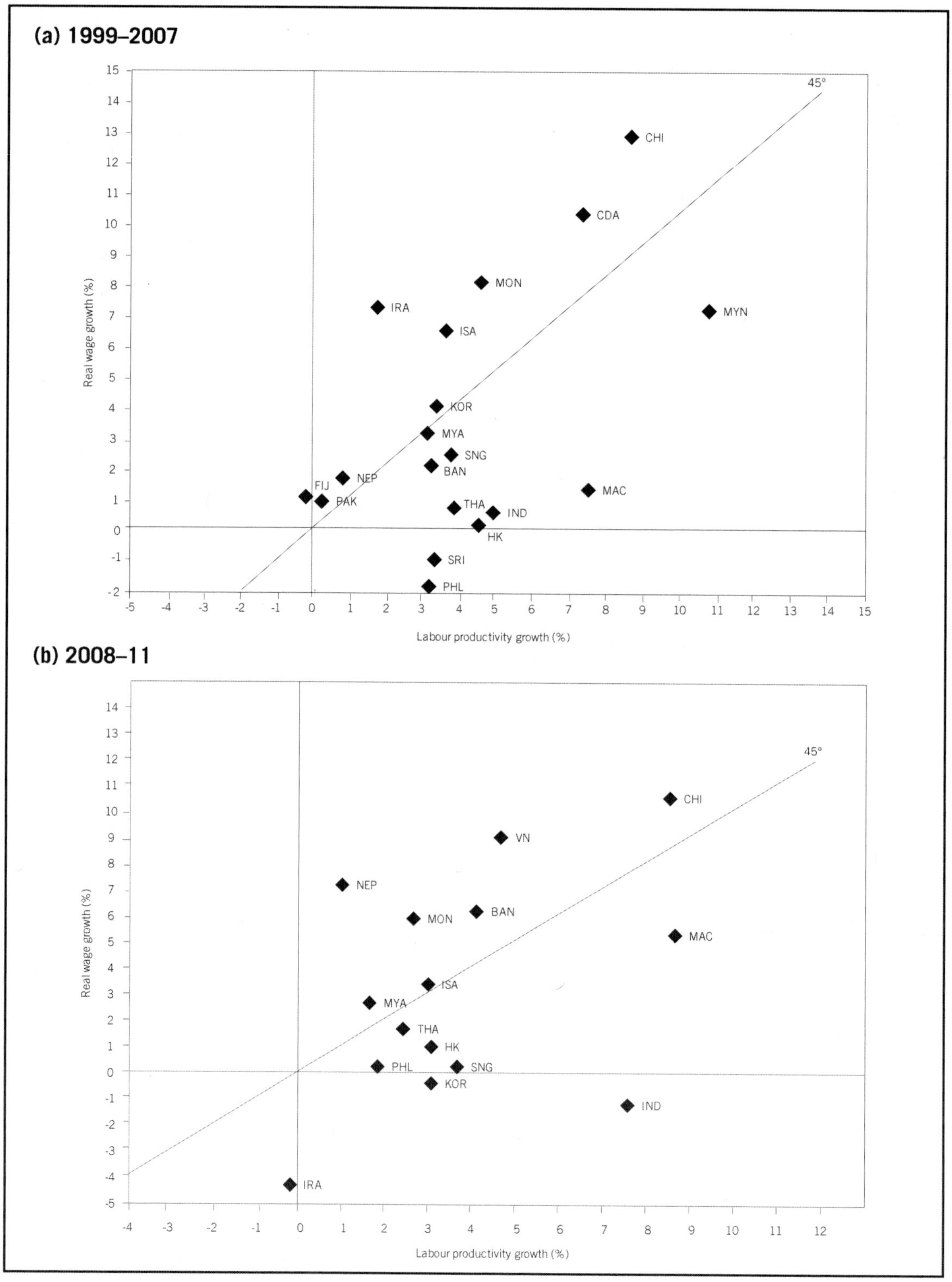

Note: If data for 1999, 2007, 2008 or 2011 were unavailable, the next closest year's data point was used to estimate the trend. For country abbreviations, see Appendix I.

Sources: ILO Trends Econometric Model, March 2012; IMF World Economic Outlook database.

3.5 Latin America and the Caribbean

Crisis withstood by robust performance

In Latin America and the Caribbean, the financial crisis interrupted a strong economic cycle. Figure 19(a) shows that during the pre-crisis years 1999–2007, average annual growth in both GDP and employment was positive and robust in a majority of countries, while figure 19(b) reflects the relatively short duration of the global crisis in this region. We see that over the period 2008–11, both GDP and employment grew at fairly solid rates in a majority of countries, in spite of the economic contraction in some major economies in 2009. Note, though, that in Central America and the Caribbean, where economies are strongly connected to the North American market, the recovery was slower than in South America.

Figure 20 covers the period between 2004, which marked the start of the continent's strong economic cycle, and 2011 – a period over which GDP grew on average by 4.4 per cent. We see that Latin America was severely affected by the global economic crisis in 2009, but rebounded rapidly in 2010, supported by the recovery in commodity prices as well as the implementation of countercyclical monetary and fiscal policies. The latter was possible as the region enjoyed a healthy fiscal situation and had reduced external debt to manageable levels during the years of expansion. What is striking is not only that the recession was short, but also that the recovery involved the creation of new jobs and led to a significant reduction in the unemployment rate, which fell from 10.3 per cent in 2004 to 6.8 per cent in 2011 (as illustrated in figure 20).

Positive figures explained by data from Brazil

These economic trends are also reflected in the wage data. Regional estimates (in figure 7) show that in Latin America and the Caribbean average real wages grew in all years between 2006 and 2011, in spite of the crisis in 2009. As in Asia, the lowest real wage growth occurred in 2008 as a result of a peak in inflation, reflecting increases in international prices of foodstuffs and oil. On the contrary, in 2009 international prices fell significantly as a result of the international slowdown, on average halving inflation in the region. This significant reduction in inflation slightly improved the purchasing power of wages, despite the economic contraction.

Overall, these regional wage trends in Latin America and the Caribbean are heavily influenced by large countries such as Brazil, where wage growth remained positive throughout the period (see figure 21).[12] Looking at the performance of a group of 14 countries for which we have full information for the period 2005–10, we observe that many other countries experienced some deterioration in their real wages in 2008 and again in 2010. Real wages contracted in ten out of 14 countries in 2008, while in 2010 there were six countries where this occurred. In both years, the majority of countries where real wages fell were in Central America and the Caribbean, as their economies are more dependent on the economic situation in the United States.

Figure 19 Growth in output and employment in Latin America and the Caribbean, 1997–2007 and 2008–11 (%)

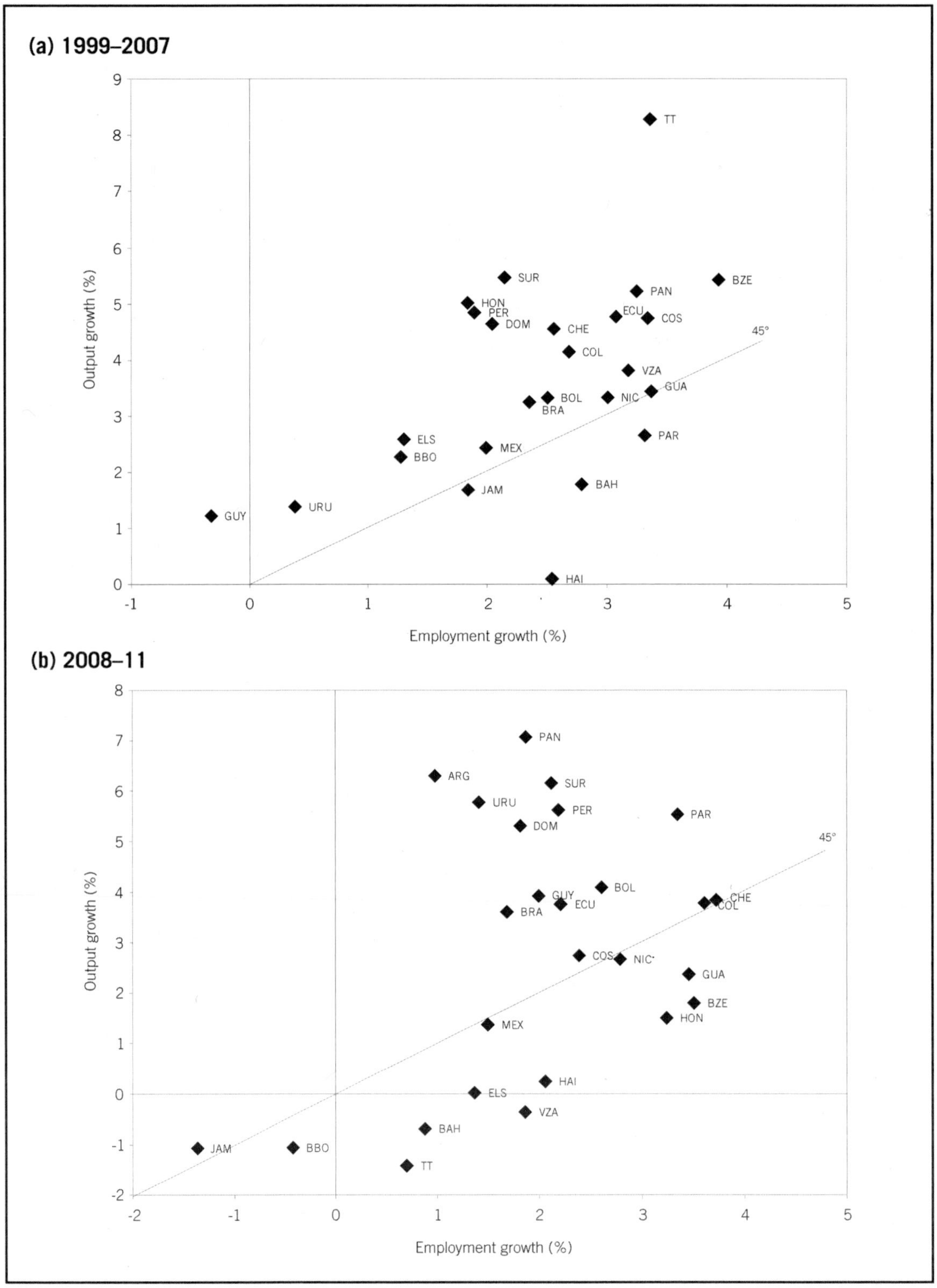

Note: For country abbreviations, see Appendix I.

Sources: ILO Trends Econometric Model, March 2012; IMF World Economic Outlook database.

Figure 20 Economic growth and unemployment in Latin America and the Caribbean, 2004–11 (%)

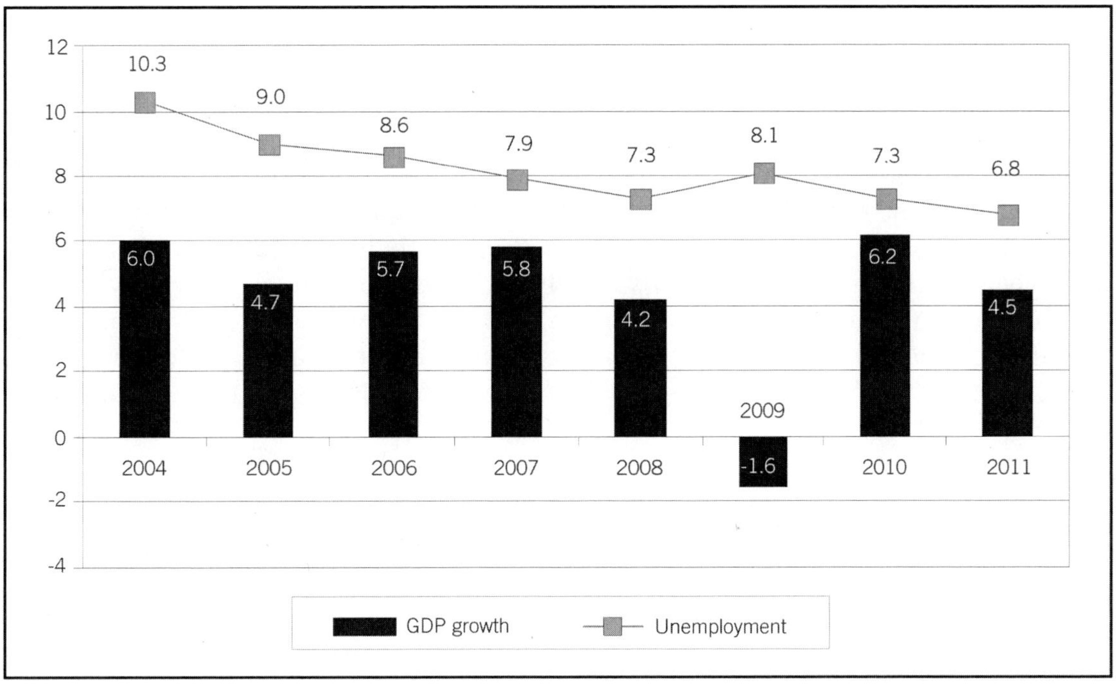

Sources: IMF World Economic Outlook database; ILO, 2011e.

Figure 21 Annual average real wage growth in Brazil, 2006–11

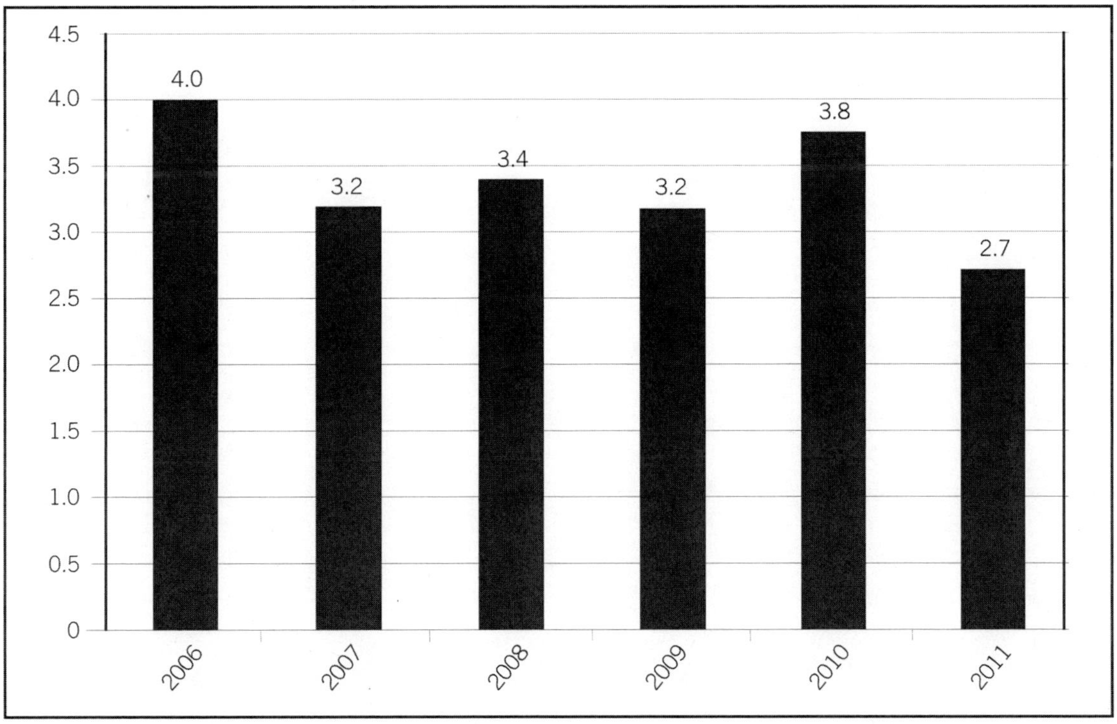

Source: ILO Global Wage Database.

Productivity up, employment up, wages up – but not everywhere

Figure 22 provides data on the annual growth of average real monthly wages during the period 2004–11, which covers the years of strong economic growth and for which consistent wage data are available for a relatively large number of countries. We see that, overall, the countries with high labour productivity growth also showed a substantial increase in real wages. So for example, average real wages grew at over 3 per cent per annum in Brazil, Peru and Uruguay, and at over 2 per cent per annum in Chile and Costa Rica. In the overwhelming majority of these countries, the unemployment rate declined, meaning that labour market indicators generally improved. Conversely, countries where GDP per capita grew only slowly during this period also saw only modest improvements (as in Honduras and Mexico) or even reductions (as in Nicaragua and El Salvador) in real wages. Three countries where good economic performance was not reflected in average real wage growth are Colombia, the Dominican Republic and Panama.

Figure 22 Growth in wages and labour productivity in selected Latin American and Caribbean countries, 2004–11 (%)

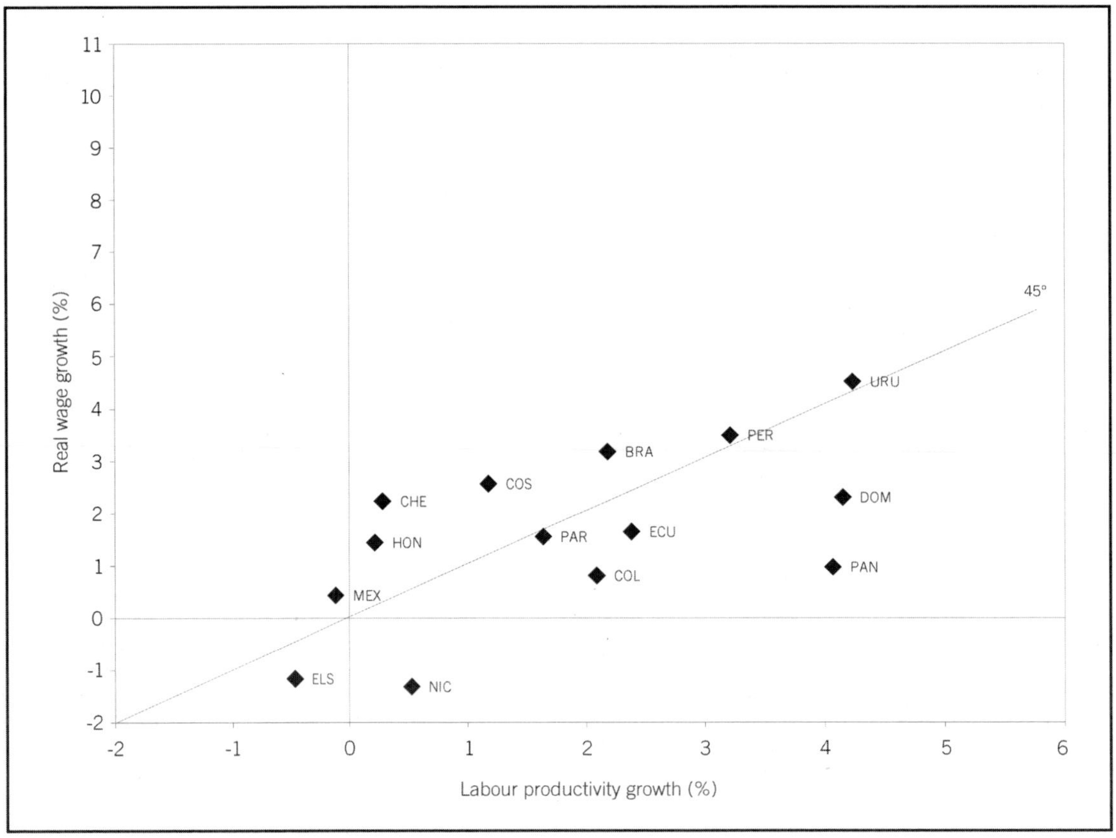

Note: If data for 2004 or 2011 were unavailable, the next closest year's data point was used to estimate the trend. For country abbreviations, see Appendix I.
Sources: ILO Global Wage Database; ILO Trends Econometric Model, March 2012.

3.6 The Middle East

Declining trade saps demand for migrant workers

The global economic crisis had the effect of initially slowing down economic growth in most countries in the Middle East (figure 23). The main impact of the crisis in this region took the form of declining international trade. There was a sharp drop in the demand for exports from less developed Middle East economies, and a temporary fall in 2009 of the value of exports for oil producers in the countries of the Gulf Cooperation Council (GCC),[13] after which oil prices and government spending both increased. In the GCC countries, where expatriate workers far outnumber native workers, the slowdown in employment growth was perhaps only temporary (though statistical information is lacking), with the exception of the Emirate of Dubai where the economic downturn appears to have translated into a reduced demand for migrant workers, particularly in construction. Migration issues are also prominent for other Middle Eastern countries, with many Syrians working in the construction sector in Lebanon, or a majority of workers in the Jordanian apparel industry coming from South Asia.

Statistical challenges

The effects of the global crisis on wages in this region are difficult to assess, for at least two reasons. First, few countries publish regular wage statistics. The only country in the Middle East to produce quarterly surveys on wages is the Kingdom of Bahrain, whose Labour Market Regulatory Authority publishes estimated average basic wages of all employees, compiled from a combination of household surveys and administrative data. By contrast, Saudi Arabia publishes annual data from its Annual Economic Survey of Establishments with a two-year lag, meaning that the most recent statistics available at the time of writing of this report were for the year 2009. Also, the wage statistics in the region are sometimes of questionable quality, though some improvements are being made in this respect: Tunisia, for example, conducted its first wage survey with the assistance of the ILO in 2011. Nevertheless, such data as are available suggest that in a majority of Middle Eastern countries wages have not increased very much, or perhaps even declined, during the past few years (figure 24).

Another complication arises with interpretation of the wage data, because average wages can hide tremendous differences between those of native workers and those of migrant workers, whose respective wages are the outcomes of very different systems of wage determination. In the GCC economies, large differences in wages between expatriate and native workers are the combined result of "Arabization" processes, which seek to increase the proportion of local workers in the private sector; the sponsorship system, which restricts the free movement of migrant workers between jobs; and public employment policies, which generate jobs that are exclusively directed at local people and offer wages that in many cases are higher than those available in the private sector. In fact, the low participation rate of women in the labour market together with the high proportion of women working in public sector jobs sometimes results in a negative gender pay gap (a situation where women earn more than men). This was the case, for example, in Syria, where in 2010 only about 13 per cent of

Figure 23 Growth in output and employment in the Middle East, 1999–2007 and 2008–11 (%)

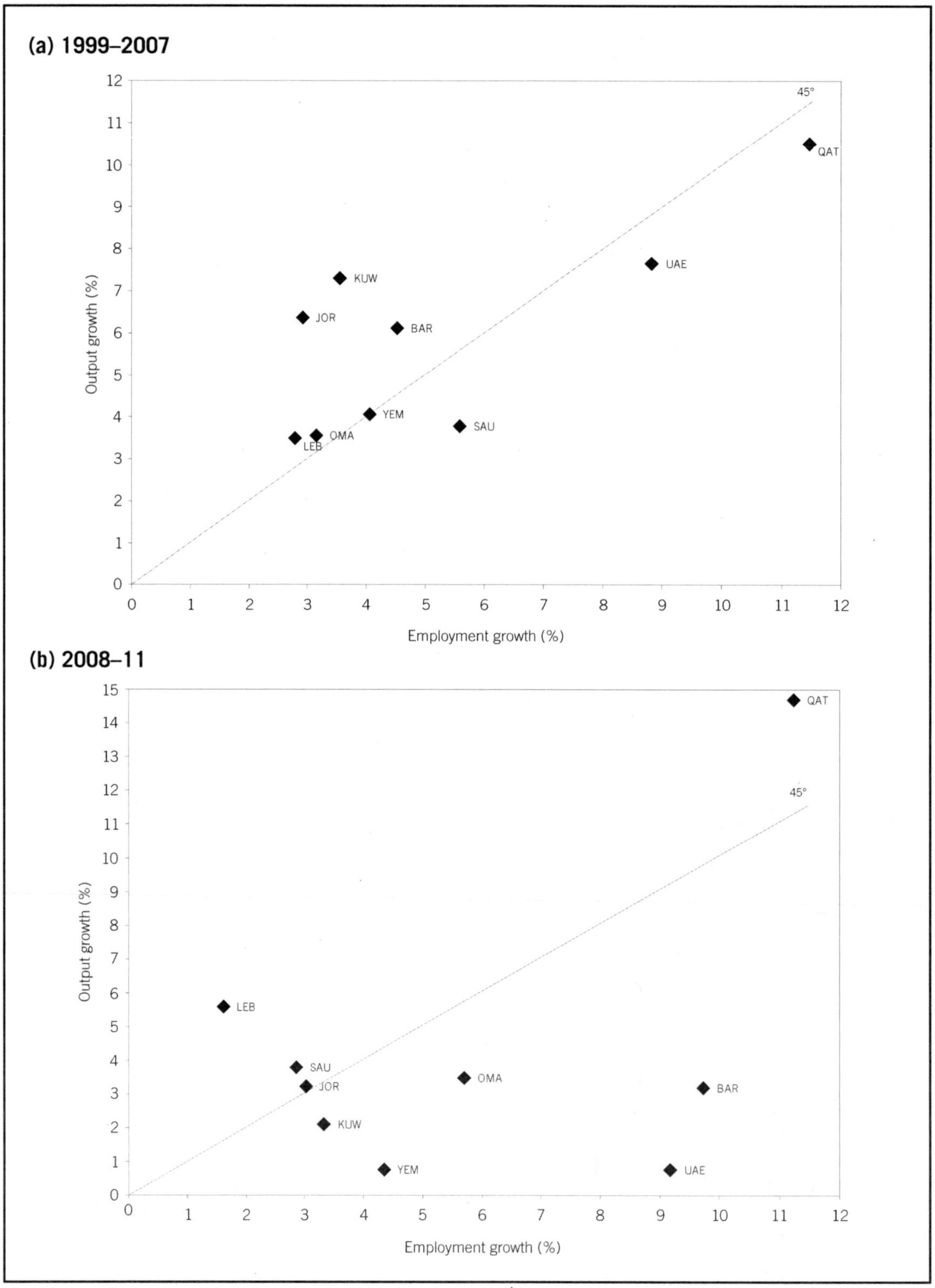

Note: For country abbreviations, see Appendix I.

Sources: ILO Trends Econometric Model, March 2012; and IMF World Economic Outlook database.

women were economically active, but where about 74 per cent of women in paid employment worked in the public sector, where wages were about 1.5 times those prevailing in the private sector (see Syrian Arab Republic, Central Bureau of Statistics, 2011a, b).

The Arab Spring: Local workers and migrant remittances

Findings from surveys show that "fair pay" and high costs of living are top priorities among young people in the Arab region (ASDA'A, 2012), and the Arab Spring seems to have prompted several countries to make further increases in wages for local people working in the public sector. Yet when it comes to the private sector, minimum wages and collective bargaining are underdeveloped in the Arab region. This has several unintended consequences including asymmetric bargaining power between workers and employers and the possibility of social and political unrest. Although remittances from GCC countries seem to have remained more resilient than expected, other destination countries may have passed the cost of the crisis onto migrant workers. In countries that are net senders of migrants, drops in remittances severely affect household incomes, with repercussions in the form of reduced aggregate consumption and savings, increasing rates of unemployment and a drop in the country's own wages (World Bank, 2011).

Figure 24 Growth in wages and labour productivity in the Middle East, 1999–2011 (%)

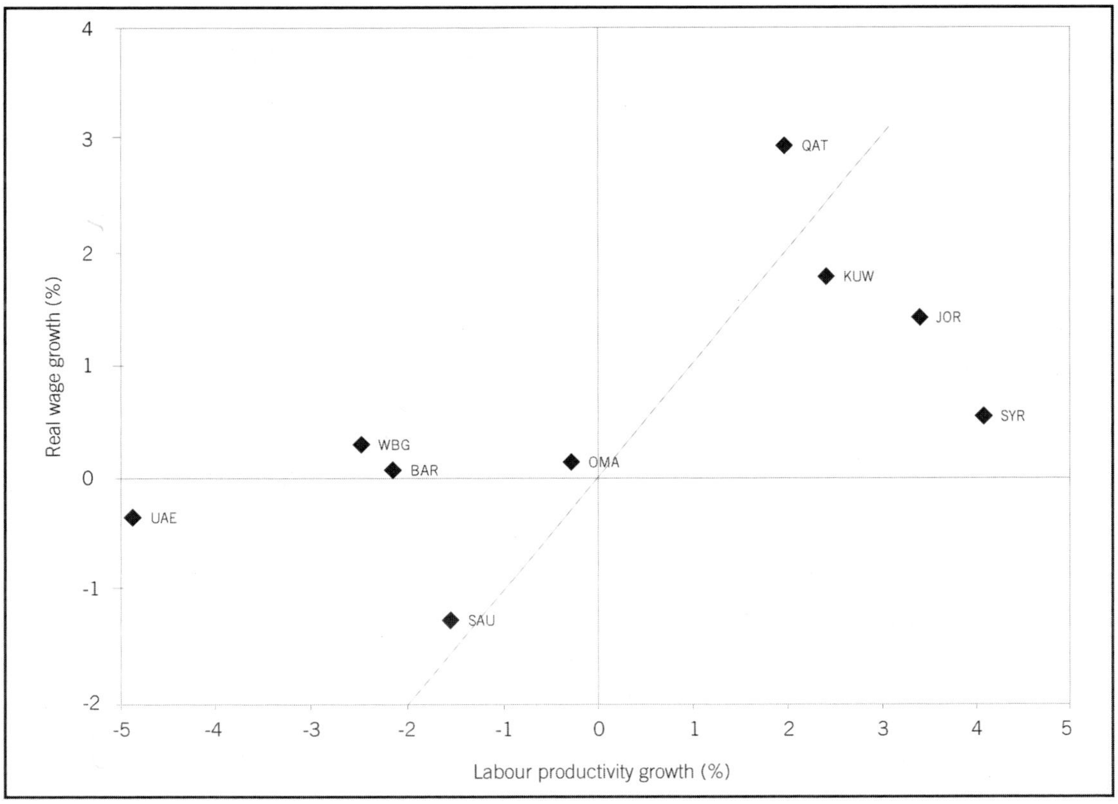

Note: If data for 1999 or 2011 were unavailable, the next closest year's data point was used to estimate the trend. For country abbreviations, see Appendix I.
Sources: ILO Global Wage Database; ILO Trends Econometric Model, March 2012.

3.7 Africa

Transition and turbulence

In the years before the crisis, Africa went through a period of relatively rapid economic growth, with annual growth rates of around 6.5 per cent over the period 2004–08. During the years 2008–11 the economic environment deteriorated, and North African countries in particular faced both external and internal challenges. External challenges arose from the close economic connection with the depressed European economies, while internal challenges reflected the radical changes and political transitions towards more democratic regimes in Egypt, Tunisia and Libya. In the short run, this period of transition has been associated with reduced flows of foreign investment and trade, and also falling tourism. Figure 25, which plots output and employment growth, shows how severely Libya's economy was affected during the period 2008–11.

Unemployment: An unaffordable luxury for most

Figure 25 (a) highlights the extent to which, in the period 1999–2007, output growth exceeded employment growth in a large number of countries, leading to sometimes substantial gains in labour productivity. An earlier study estimated the annual growth rate of labour productivity in sub-Saharan Africa at 1.9 per cent per annum over the period 2000–09 (ILO, 2010b). But here again, as emphasized in the section above on Asia, in poor developing countries employment growth often follows growth in the working-age population, as unemployment benefits are underdeveloped and most people just cannot afford to remain unemployed. For this reason we also show (in figure 26) how GDP growth related to the growth of paid employment in Africa. Here we see that economic growth was accompanied by relatively strong increases in the number of paid employees.

Limited data show moderate wage increases

How have these developments affected wages? Data on the evolution of average wages in Africa are relatively scarce. Only a few countries in Africa, including Botswana, Egypt, Lesotho, Mauritius, South Africa and Uganda, carry out quarterly or annual establishment surveys of the kind conducted by developed countries in order to measure the evolution of earnings. Morocco publishes an index of nominal average wages, compiled on the basis of earnings reported to the Caisse Nationale de Sécurité Sociale, its social security institution. In the majority of remaining countries, wage data are at best collected through labour force surveys that are implemented at irregular intervals, and are not always comparable across years. Our tentative regional estimate in figure 7 shows that wage growth since 2006 has generally been moderate, with the exception of 2010 when regional average wages increased considerably, mostly owing to the large weight of South Africa in the regional estimate. Figure 27 shows the real wage growth and labour productivity growth between 1999 and 2011 for selected countries. In 2010, according to official figures, real average wages increased by nearly 10 per cent in South Africa, where wage growth remains unequally distributed.

Figure 25 Growth in output and employment in Africa, 1999–2007 and 2008–11 (%)

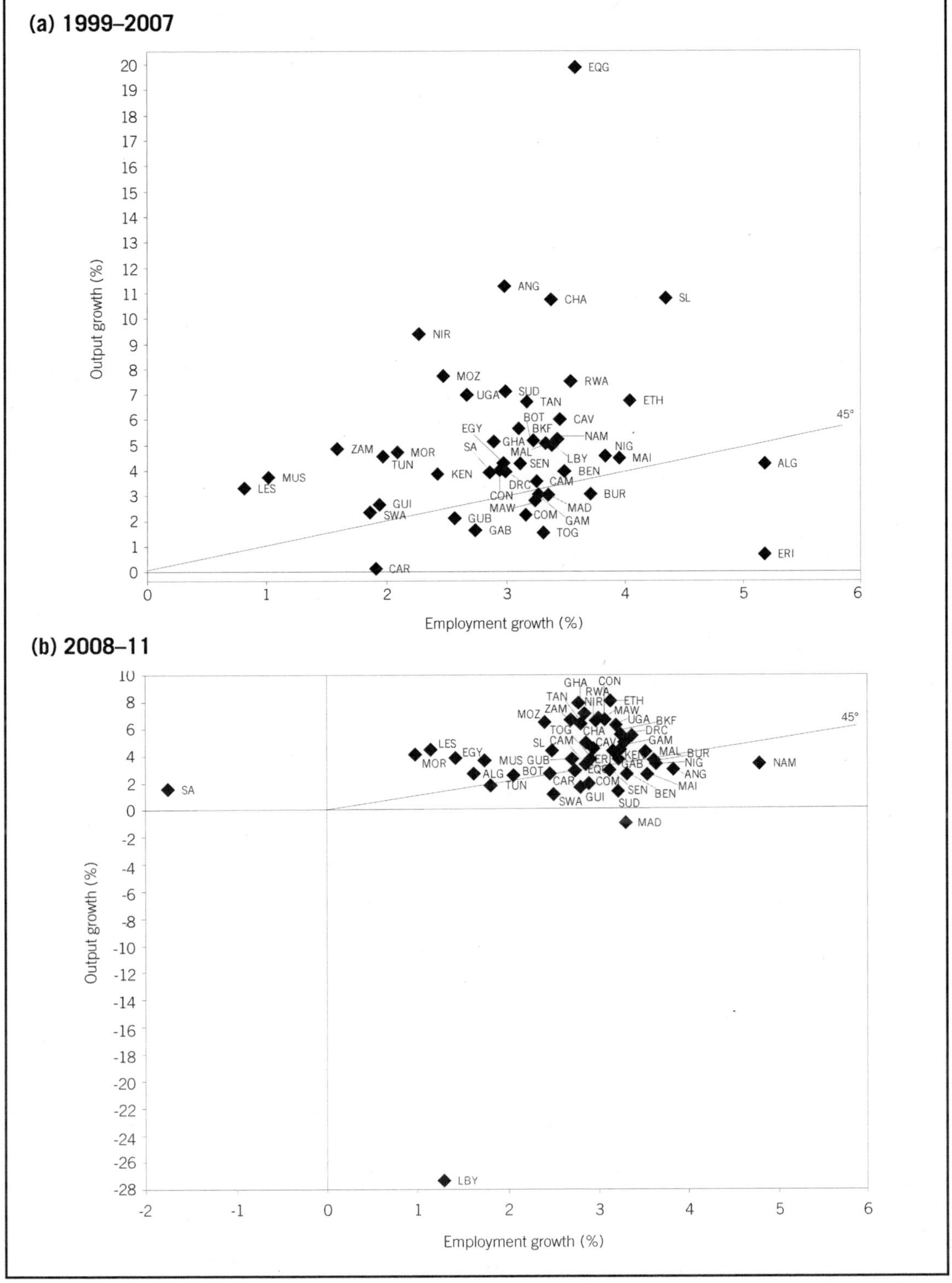

Note: For country abbreviations, see Appendix I.

Sources: ILO Trends Econometric Model, March 2012; IMF World Economic Outlook database.

Figure 26 Growth in output and numbers of paid employees in Africa, 1999–2007 and 2008–11 (%)

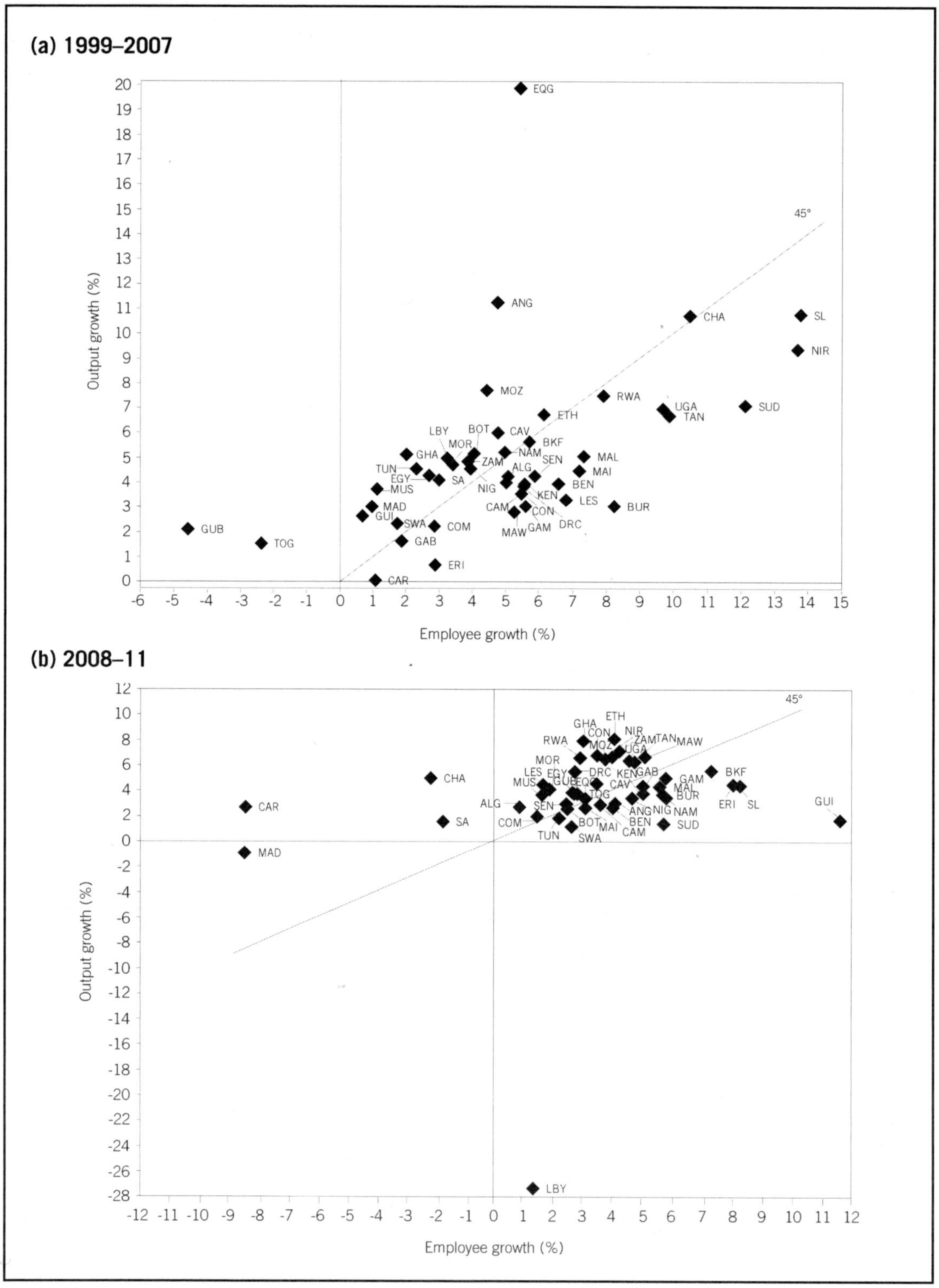

Note: For country abbreviations, see Appendix I.

Sources: ILO Trends Econometric Model, March 2012; IMF World Economic Outlook database.

Figure 27 Growth in wages and labour productivity in selected African countries, 1999–2011 (%)

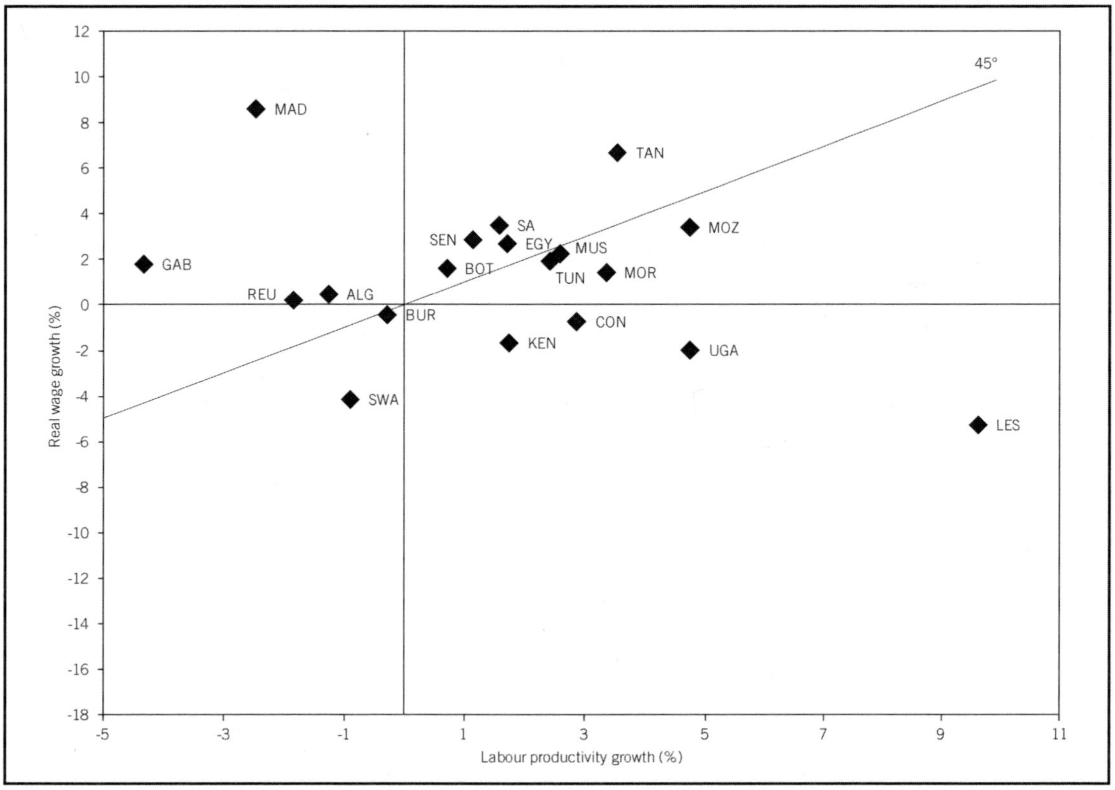

Note: If data for 1999 or 2011 were unavailable, the next closest year's data point was used to estimate the trend. For country abbreviations, see Appendix I.
Sources: ILO Global Wage Database; ILO Trends Econometric Model, March 2012.

4 Minimum wages and the working poor

In current economic conditions, minimum wages remain a topic of debate on the policy agenda and in the public domain in both developed and developing countries. As part of its Decent Work Agenda, the ILO encourages member States to adopt a minimum wage to reduce working poverty and provide social protection for vulnerable employees.[14] ILO standards further recommend that minimum wages should be set by authorities after consultation with social partners, and that a balanced approach should be adopted which takes into account the needs of workers and their families as well as economic factors, including levels of productivity, the requirements of economic development and the need to maintain a high level of employment.[15] Along the same lines, the European Commission recently expressed the view that Member States should establish "decent and sustainable wages" and that "setting minimum wages at appropriate levels can help prevent growing in-work poverty and is an important factor in ensuring decent job quality" (see European Commission 2012a, p. 9). Debates continue regarding the level at which minimum wages should be set.

4.1 Developed economies

Different mechanisms, different perceptions

Among developed economies, minimum wages vary substantially as a proportion of full-time median earnings, ranging from about 60 per cent in New Zealand and France to less than 40 per cent in Japan, Spain and the United States (figure 28). The differences in the levels of minimum wages among countries reflect the different institutional mechanisms through which levels are determined (Lee, 2012). They also reflect different perceptions about the risks that minimum wages may pose in respect of the displacement of low-paid workers or the number of jobs available in the labour market. These factors, alongside variations in average wages, also partly explain why the absolute level of the minimum wage varies so widely across developed economies (figure 28).

Just as perceptions about the optimal level of the minimum wage diverge, so do views about the role of this policy instrument during periods of economic crisis. Focusing on developed economies only, it appears that policy-makers actively used the minimum wage as a social protection tool for the most vulnerable workers at the beginning of the crisis through 2009 (see figure 29). However, in later years the minimum wage was in most cases only adjusted with a view to compensating for inflation; this can be seen in figure 29, where in the years after 2009 real minimum wages grew in developed economies by considerably less (or even declined).

Crisis response brings compulsory cuts

In Greece, the minimum wage has been severely cut, losing 22 per cent of its previous value[16] (the value in figure 28 refers to the minimum wage before this adjustment). This change was made on the request of the European Central Bank, the European Commission and the IMF as a condition for giving the Greek Government access to bailout funds from the European Financial Stability Facility (EFSF). According to the IMF (IMF, 2012c), wage cuts were necessary if the country was to regain competitiveness and growth, ends that could not be achieved through national currency devaluations or interest rate adjustments. The IMF also considered that the minimum wage in Greece was substantially higher than in other developed economies, even though the statistics presented in figure 28 suggest it was not out of range. In Portugal, access to the EFSF came at the condition of a minimum wage freeze.

4.2 Developing and emerging economies

Minimum wages are also widely used in developing and emerging economies, although here information about the levels at which they are set relative to median or average wages is more difficult to obtain (given that information on average wages is often based on a narrow subset of paid employees in the formal economy or in urban areas). A recent study, however, showed that, just as in developed economies, the extent of minimum wage adjustments during the crisis varied among both low-income and middle-income countries. The joint ILO–World Bank inventory of policy responses to the financial and economic crisis found that 22 out of the 55 low- and middle-income countries surveyed reported changes in the minimum wage over the period from mid-2008 to the end of 2010.[17]

Figure 28 Minimum wage levels in selected developed economies, in PPP$ and as a share of median full-time wage, 2010

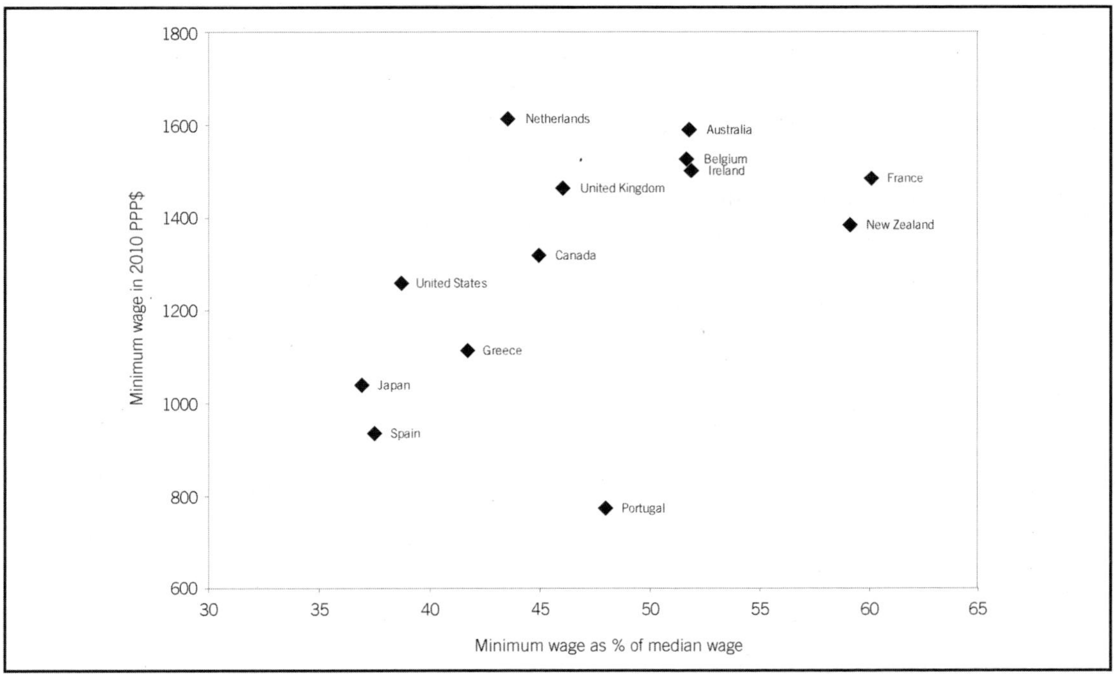

Notes: If the 8 per cent supplement for holiday pay is included, the minimum/median wage ratio amounts to 47.1 per cent in the Netherlands. If 13th and 14th months' salary is included, the minimum/median wage ratio amounts to 56 per cent in Portugal and 43.8 per cent in Spain.

Sources: ILO Global Wage Database; Low Pay Commission, 2012.

Figure 29 Minimum wage growth in developed economies, 2006–11

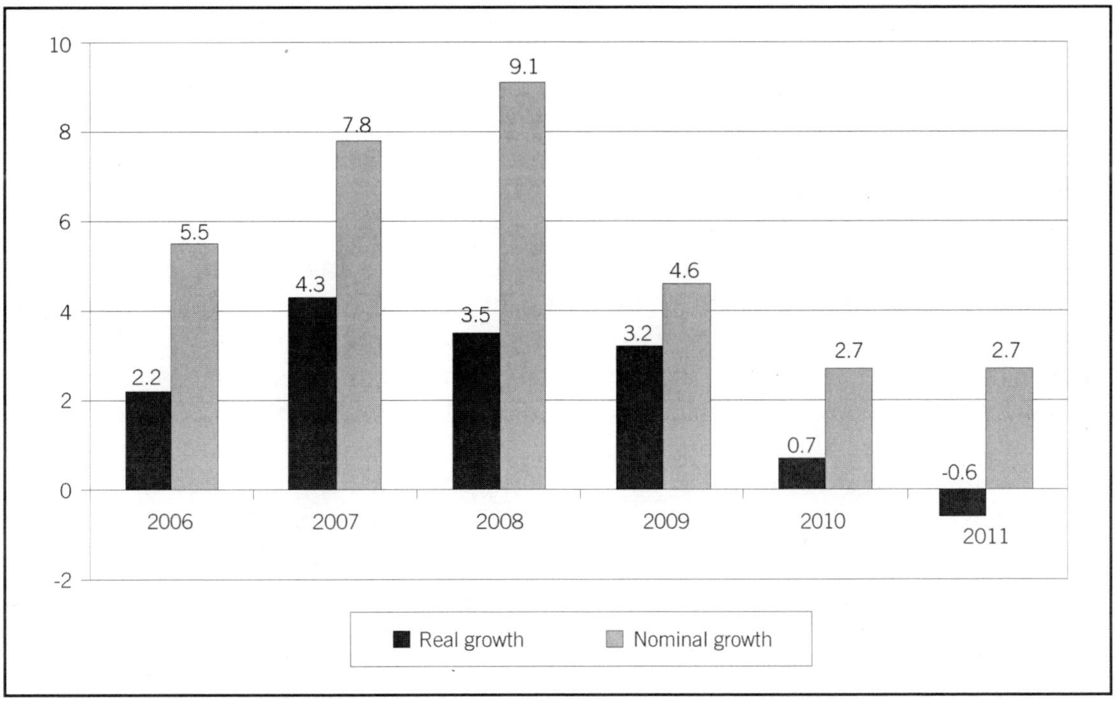

Note: Based on a non-weighted simple average of estimated growth rates of real and nominal minimum wages including 26 developed economies.

Source: ILO Global Wage Database.

Waged work and privilege in developing countries

A reservation frequently advanced about minimum wages in developing countries is that all wage-earners belong to an elite group, which enjoys higher standards of living and privileges not accessible to others such as the self-employed or those involved in family work. While it is true that waged employment is typically associated with higher-productivity activities, superior employment conditions and greater rights at work as compared with own-account or contributing family work, many waged and salaried workers in developing countries are in fact living with their families in poverty, as discussed in box 1. Figure 30 provides estimates of the share of waged and salaried workers living below the US$1.25 and US$2 international poverty lines for 32 developing countries. These estimates imply that out of a total number of approximately 209 million wage earners who worked in these 32 developing countries at different points in time from 1997 to 2006, about 23 million were earning below US$1.25 a day and 64 million were earning less than US$2 per day. This indicates that minimum wages, in spite of their limitations, remain a relevant tool for povery reduction.

One country in Latin America where the minimum wage has had a significant impact is Brazil. Although the minimum wage revaluation strategy has been pursued for about 20 years, it has accelerated since 2005, when, as part of a strategy to foster domestic consumption, regular adjustments were systematically linked to inflation plus GDP growth. This same strategy was followed even during the financial crisis years when wage policy was part of a countercyclical strategy. By contrast, in Mexico the minimum wage has increased only very modestly in real terms between 2005 and 2011, as the minimum wage policy has been strongly determined by efforts to achieve a fiscal balance (as minimum wages determine many social security benefits) and increase export competitiveness. As a result, minimum wages are below market levels, even for unskilled workers. These two cases illustrate the different approaches towards minimum wages.

Asia has experienced several developments in the realm of minimum wage growth and minimum wage setting. Across the region, minimum wage growth has been positive in almost all countries since 2005. This growth has been coupled with positive economic growth and solid real average wage growth over the same period (see figure 15). At the same time, all of these factors have occurred alongside growth in the share of employees in total employment and hence the proportion of workers that can be directly affected by a minimum wage. For instance, in China progress has been made towards improving enforcement and coordination among provinces in terms of minimum wage-fixing. Other examples include Mongolia, which improved its minimum wage setting mechanism by including social partners; Malaysia, which announced a first-time minimum wage in 2012; and the Philippines, which simplified its complex minimum wage system. In India, minimum wages paid through the National Rural Employment Generation Scheme (NREGS) appear to have reduced non-compliance with minimum wages in the private sector (Rani and Belser, 2012).

Minimum wages in the Middle East largely declined between 2005 and 2011 and, generally, are a limited policy tool within the region. While employees represented about 66 per cent of total employment in 2011, the legal coverage of minimum wages is often more restricted, if a minimum wage exists at all. For instance, in some countries the minimum wage is restricted to the national population or discriminates against migrant workers who receive lower rates. In other cases, the minimum wage may only apply to the public sector, as is the case in Bahrain.

Box 1 Poverty among waged and salaried workers

The working poor are defined as employed members of households living below a defined poverty line (see Kapsos and Horne, 2011). For international comparisons, the PPP-adjusted poverty lines of US$1.25 or US$2 a day are typically used to determine extreme and moderate poverty, respectively; households with daily per capita consumption below these lines are classified as poor.[18] Extreme poverty among workers in developing countries is often associated with subsistence activities – for example, own-account workers or contributing family workers operating in small-scale agricultural work. There is indeed evidence to back up the association between the working poor and subsistence agriculture: a recent ILO study found that in 53 countries with available data from national household surveys, four out of five workers in extreme poverty (below the US$1.25 poverty line) were living in rural areas, and that 68 per cent of the working poor were employed in the agricultural sector (see Kapsos and Horne, 2011).

Yet data from many of the same surveys indicate that a narrow focus on poverty among own-account and contributing family workers would substantially undercount the extent of working poverty in developing countries. Figure 30 shows that in Madagascar, for example, more than 80 per cent of waged and salaried workers were poor in 2005, with more than half living in extreme poverty. In Mozambique, Burundi and Tajikistan, over 60 per cent of employees were living in poverty, and in Cambodia, the Republic of the Congo and Pakistan over 50 per cent of employees were poor, according to the most recent survey data.

How do these figures compare with the incidence of poverty among own-account workers and contributing family workers? Across the 32 countries, the share of poor own-account and contributing family workers exceeds that of poor wage earners in all but two countries (Pakistan and Tajikistan). In many countries, therefore, having a waged or salaried job is associated with a lower probability of being poor than for own-account or contributing family workers. However, in some countries, being in waged employment does not convey large advantages in terms of the likelihood of being poor versus the other employment categories. For instance, in Cambodia 56.5 per cent of employees were living below the US$2 poverty line in 2004, versus 65.8 per cent of own-account workers and unpaid family workers.

In addition, poor waged and salaried workers often make up a large share of the overall working poor in developing countries. In Indonesia in 2002, the number of wage earners living below the US$2 poverty line was estimated at 15.5 million, versus 29.4 million poor own-account and contributing family workers – amounting to more than five poor waged and salaried workers for every ten poor own-account and unpaid family workers. In Pakistan in 2005, there were eight wage earners living in extreme poverty for every ten poor own-account and unpaid family workers. Thus, while the working poor in developing countries are indeed disproportionately engaged in agricultural activities in rural areas, policies aimed at improving productivity and raising the earnings and welfare of the poor must also take into consideration the large numbers of waged and salaried workers living with their families in poverty.

Box 1 Poverty among waged and salaried workers (continued)

Figure 30 Employed working poor (earning below US$1.25 and US$2 a day), as % of total employees

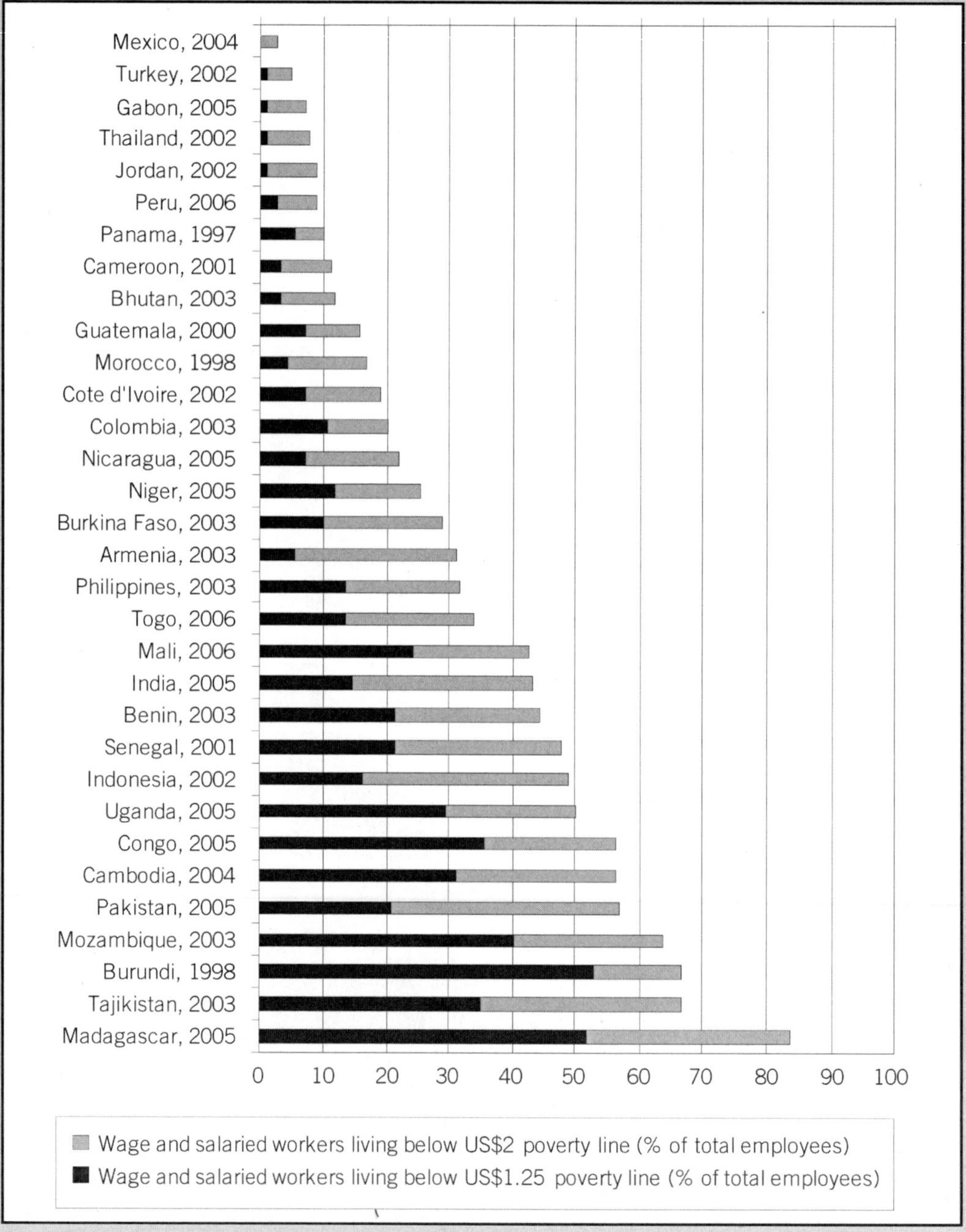

Source: ILO calculations based on national household survey data.

Source: Steven Kapsos, Labour Economist, ILO.

PART II — Falling labour shares and equitable growth

Recent trends in wages and productivity growth determine what is known as the *functional distribution of national income* – that is, the distribution of national income between labour and capital. When overall GDP grows faster than total labour compensation, the labour income share (also called the "wage share") falls relative to the capital income share. By contrast, when the growth in total labour compensation exceeds the growth in total GDP, the labour income share increases and the capital income share falls. In this part of the report we analyse trends in the labour income share and the causes behind the trends, contributing to the recently growing literature on the subject.[19]

We then ask how changes in the labour income share have affected macroeconomic aggregates such as consumption, investment and net exports. In the current global economic context, understanding the causal relationship between labour compensation and aggregate demand is of paramount importance. The macroeconomic effects of changes in labour shares have so far received relatively less attention in the empirical literature, even though wages are widely perceived as having a major impact on the economy. Our empirical analysis contributes towards the existing literature by providing a statistical causal framework and by covering both developed and developing countries.

5 The fall in the labour income share

5.1 Trends in labour shares

A myth of stability exploded

During much of the past century, a stable labour income share was accepted as a natural corollary or "stylized fact" of economic growth. As industrial countries became more prosperous, the total incomes both of workers and of capital owners grew at almost exactly the same rate, and the division of national income between labour and capital therefore remained constant over long periods of time, with only minor fluctuations.[20] It seemed as if some unwritten law of economics would ensure that labour and capital would benefit equally from material progress, and the subject of the functional distribution of income almost vanished from the agenda of academic research. In recent years, however, this long-held conventional wisdom has been challenged. An outpouring of literature has provided consistent new empirical evidence indicating that recent decades have seen a downward trend for the labour share in a majority of countries for which data are available.

The OECD has observed, for example, that over the period from 1990 to 2009 the share of labour compensation in national income declined in 26 out of 30 developed economies for which data were available, and calculated that the median labour share of national income across these countries fell considerably from 66.1 per cent to 61.7 per cent (OECD, 2012b). These findings echo the evidence presented in the ILO *Global Wage Report 2010/11*, which described declining wage shares in a large majority of OECD countries since 1980 (ILO, 2010a; see also ILO, 2008a). Earlier, similar trends had been observed in other reports published by international organisations (IMF, 2007; European Commission, 2007; BIS, 2006; ILO, 2008a, 2010a; OECD, 2011, 2012a). Looking beyond the advanced economies, the ILO *World of Work Report 2011* found that the decline in the labour income share was even more pronounced in many emerging and developing countries, with considerable declines in Asia and North Africa and more stable but still declining wage shares in Latin America (IILS, 2011). Other studies also point to the apparently global nature of this trend, suggesting a decline in the proportion of worldwide income going into labour compensation (see ILO, 2008a; Stockhammer, forthcoming; Husson, 2010; Artus, 2009).

Evidence for labour share decline

Figures 31 and 32 illustrate the trends in so-called "adjusted" labour income shares for the period 1970 to 2007 or 2010 for certain individual and grouped developed countries and for three groups of developing and emerging economies.[21] In figure 31, we observe that the simple average of labour shares in 16 developed countries for which data are available for this long period declined from about 75 per cent of national income in the mid-1970s to about 65 per cent in the years just before the global economic and financial crisis. Figure 32 shows how the average of labour shares also declined in a group of 16 developing and emerging economies, from around 62 per cent of GDP in the early 1990s to 58 per cent just before the crisis. Even in China, a country where wages roughly tripled over the last decade (see Part I), GDP increased at a faster rate than the total wage bill – and hence the labour income share went down (figure 33). The data available for China, Kenya, the Republic of Korea, Mexico and Turkey (figure 32) suggest that the decline in this group of countries may already have started in the 1980s.

The global economic crisis seems to have reversed the decreasing trend only briefly. In developed economies, the wage share bounced back initially after the beginning of the crisis but began to decline again from 2009. This reflects the typical "countercyclical" nature of the wage share, which arises because wages tend to be less volatile than profits during economic downturns. The OECD, for example, observed: "In times of economic recession, this decline [in the wage share] has typically paused, but then subsequently resumed with a recovery. The recent economic and financial crisis and subsequent sluggish recovery have not deviated from this general pattern" (OECD, 2012b, p. 112).

Different skill levels, different impacts

These trends have not been uniform across workers with different levels of education and skills. Studies on developed economies that have disaggregated total labour compensation by categories of workers have invariably found that recent trends were driven by

Figure 31 Adjusted labour income shares in developed economies, Germany, the USA and Japan, 1970–2010

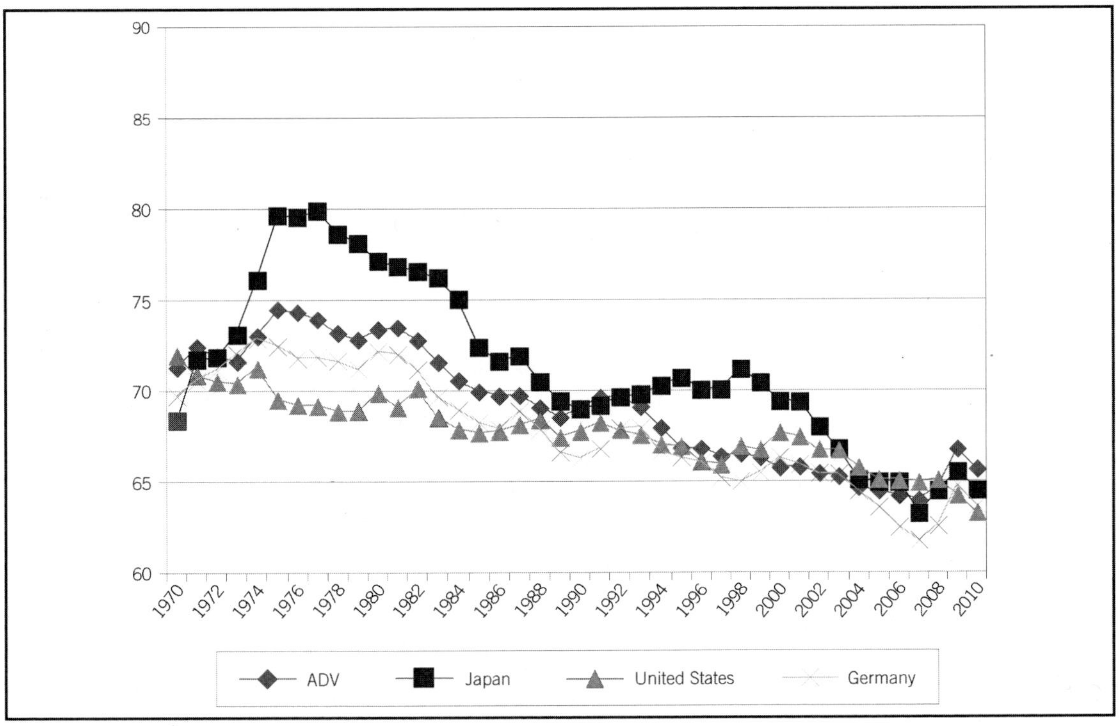

Note: ADV = unweighted average of 16 high-income OECD countries (Australia, Austria, Belgium, Canada, Denmark, Finland, France, Germany, Ireland, Italy, Japan, the Netherlands, Spain, Sweden, the United Kingdom, and the United States. The Republic of Korea is excluded.)
Source: Stockhammer, forthcoming, from AMECO database.

the falling wage shares of low- and medium-skilled workers. The International Institute for Labour Studies (IILS, 2011) calculated, for example, that in the ten developed economies for which data were available the wage share fell by 12 percentage points for low-skilled workers between the early 1980s and 2005, while it increased by 7 percentage points for highly skilled workers. Similarly, the IMF found that between 1980 and 2005 the labour share of unskilled workers fell in the United States, Japan and Europe (by 15 per cent, 15 per cent and 10 per cent respectively), but increased for skilled workers educated to tertiary level and above (by 7 per cent, 2 per cent and 8 per cent respectively) (IMF, 2007). More recently, the OECD found that in the 13 countries for which data are available, the average wage share of those with low educational levels fell (OECD 2012b). This occurred in the context of the observed polarization of jobs, with increasing numbers of low- and high-skilled jobs and fewer medium-skilled jobs. Although one could expect that an expansion of low-skilled jobs would in principle raise the wages of low-skilled workers, it appears that such workers have increasingly been displaced by overqualified workers with intermediate levels of education.

Taking out the top earners

Labour shares, as measured in the UN System of National Accounts, therefore underestimate the fall in the proportion of labour compensation going to workers paid below the median wage. If the labour compensation of the top 1 per cent of income earners

Figure 32 Adjusted labour income shares in developing and emerging economies, 1970–2007

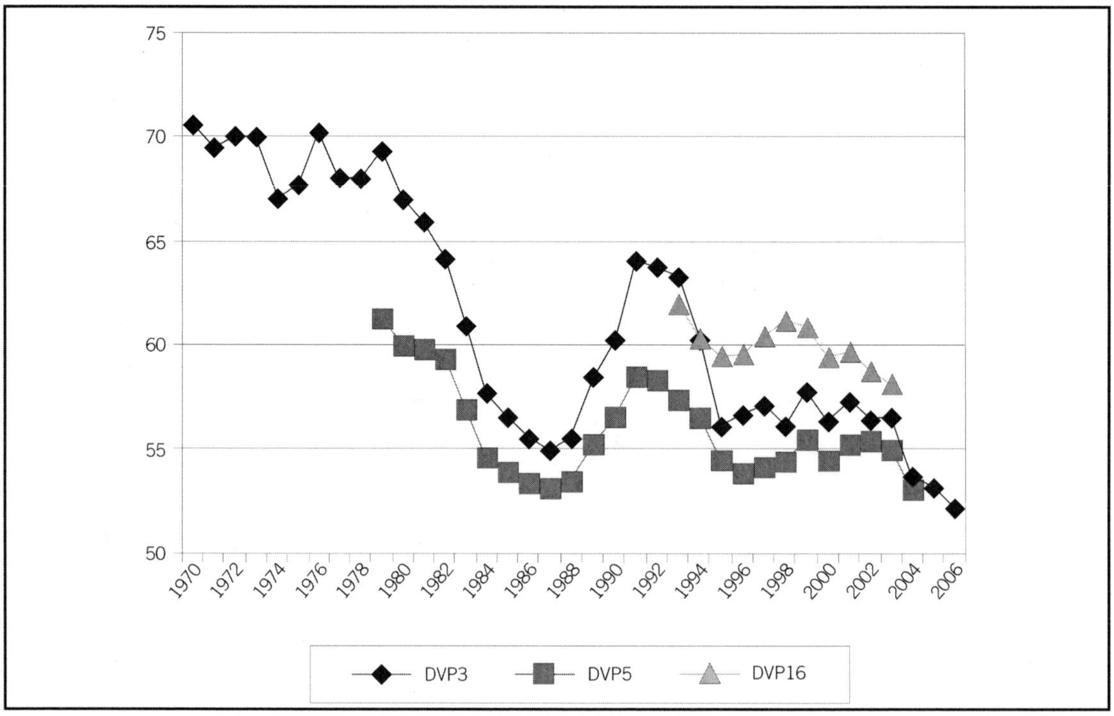

Note: DVP3 = unweighted average of Mexico, Republic of Korea and Turkey; DVP5 = unweighted average of China, Kenya, Mexico, Republic of Korea and Turkey; DVP16 = unweighted average of Argentina, Brazil, Chile, China, Costa Rica, Kenya, Mexico, Namibia, Oman, Panama, Peru, Republic of Korea, Russia, South Africa, Thailand and Turkey.
Sources: ILO Global Wage Database; Stockhammer, forthcoming.

was excluded from the computation, the drop of the labour share would appear even greater (see, for example, IILS, 2011; OECD, 2012b). This reflects the sharp increase, especially in English-speaking countries, of the wage and salaries (including bonuses and exercised stock options) of top executives, who now cohabit with capital owners at the top of the income hierarchy (see Atkinson, Piketty and Saez, 2011; Piketty and Saez, 2003; OECD, 2008; Wolff and Zacharias, 2009).[22] The proportion of wage earnings in the top segments of household income also increased, to various degrees, in other countries including Japan, the Netherlands, Canada, Italy, Spain and the United Kingdom – though not in Sweden, Finland or Australia (Atkinson, Piketty and Saez, 2011).

The other side of the coin: The increasing capital share

The mirror image of the fall in the labour share is the increase in the capital share of income (often called the profit share), which is measured most frequently as the share of gross operating surplus of corporations as a percentage of GDP. The ILO/IILS found that when total capital share is disaggregated by type of corporations, the growth of the capital share has been faster in the financial sector than for non-financial corporations. Also, in advanced economies, profits of non-financial corporations have increasingly been allocated to pay dividends, which accounted for 35 per cent of profits in 2007 (IILS, 2011) and increased pressure on companies to reduce the share of value added going to labour compensation.

Figure 33 Unadjusted labour income share in China, 1992–2008

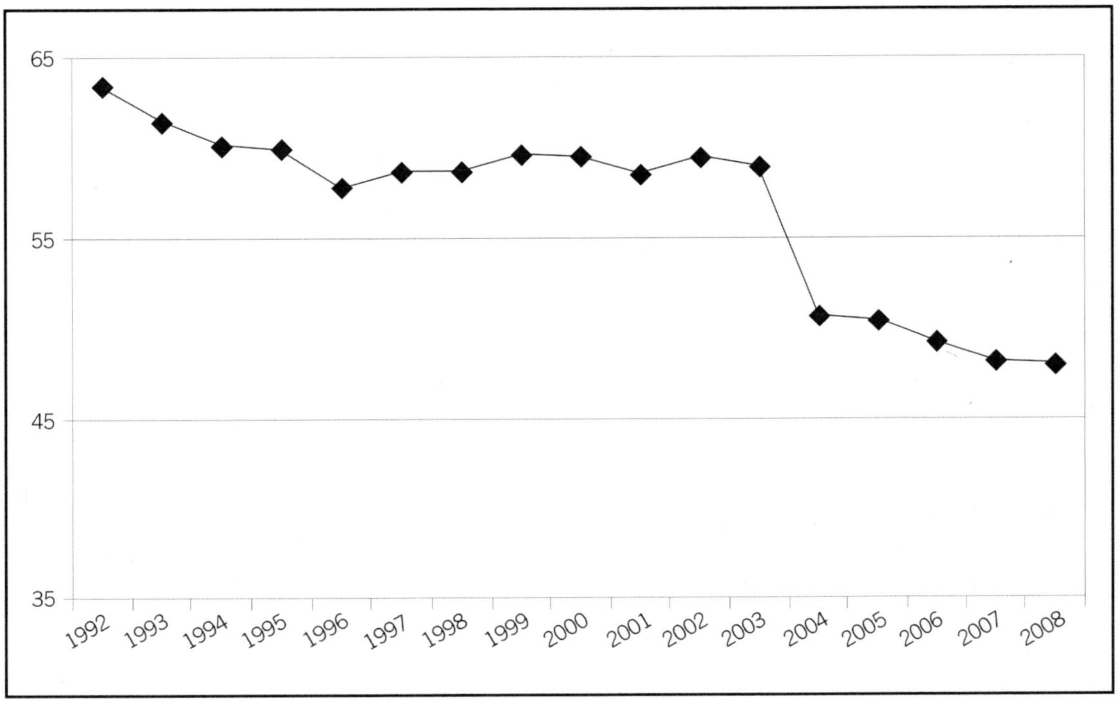

Note: The unadjusted wage share is calculated as total labour compensation of employees divided by value added. The sudden change between 2003 and 2004 likely reflects an adjustment to the data; nonetheless, it does not change the direction of the trend.
Source: ILO calculations based on data from the *China Statistical Yearbooks*, http://www.stats.gov.cn/english/statisticaldata/yearlydata/ [accessed 17 Sep. 2012].

Looking at a set of four developed economies (France, Germany, the United Kingdom and the United States), Husson found that over the period 1987–2008 a large part of the increased surplus of corporations went into boosting the dividends paid to shareholders (Husson, 2010). He calculated that in France total dividends increased from 4 per cent of the total wage bill in the early 1980s to 13 per cent in 2008. Interestingly, in the United Kingdom the shares of dividend payments and labour compensation both increased, so that the higher dividends came at the expense of reduced retained earnings.[23] In the United States, three-quarters of the increase in gross operating surplus went into the payment of dividends. Given the greater concentration of income with capital rather than labour, booming dividends have often contributed to higher overall household income inequality (OECD, 2011; see also Roine and Waldenström, 2012).

5.2 The gap between wages and productivity

The effect on the labour share

A shrinking labour share is almost always tied to another empirical regularity, namely the growing discrepancy between the respective growth rates of average wages and labour productivity (for a detailed exposition of the relationship between wages, productivity, unit labour costs and labour shares, see Appendix II). A publication by the US Bureau of Labour Statistics, for example, shows that the gap between hourly labour productivity and hourly compensation growth contributed to a decline in the labour

Figure 34 Hourly productivity and compensation in the United States, Q1 1947–Q1 2012

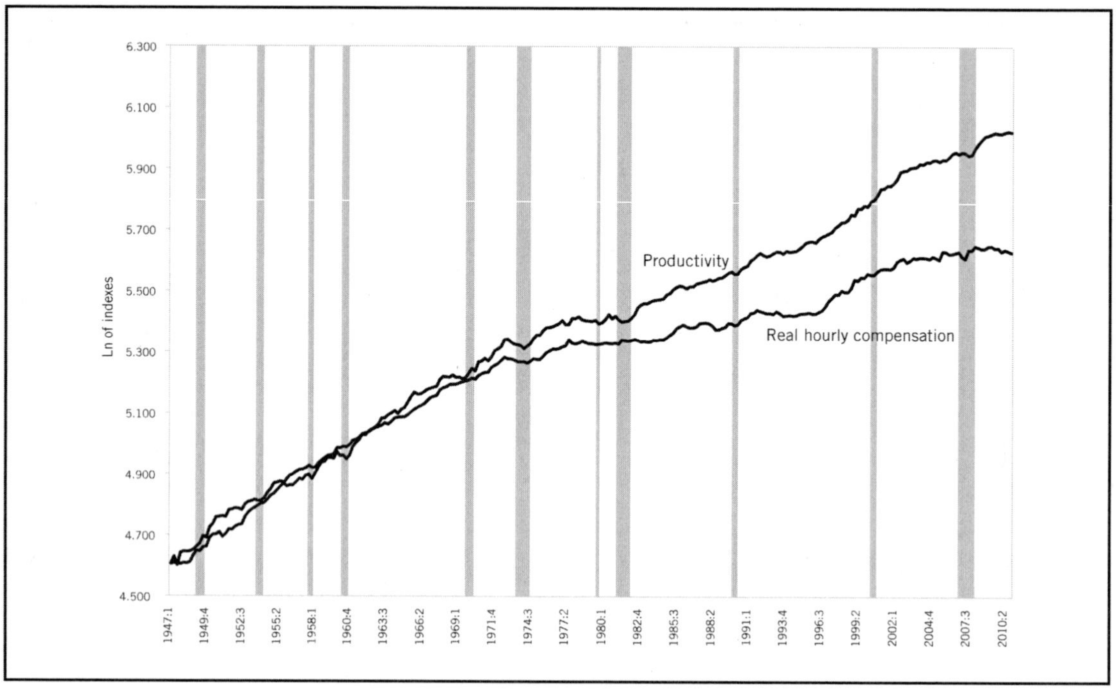

Note: Shaded areas represent recessions.

Source: Figure reproduced from Fleck, Glaser and Sprague (2011) using updated data published by the Division of Major Sector Productivity of the Bureau of Labour Statistics, as of 26 June, 2012.

share in the United States (Fleck, Glaser and Sprague, 2011). Since 1980 hourly labour productivity in the non-farm business sector increased by around 85 per cent, while real hourly compensation increased by about 35 per cent (figure 34).

Another example is Germany, where labour productivity (defined as value added per person employed) has surged by almost a quarter (22.6 per cent) over the past two decades, while real monthly wages have remained flat over the same period – indeed, between 2003 and 2011 they actually fell below the level seen in the mid-1990s (see figure 35(a)). The decline in monthly wages is attributable in part to a sharp reduction in monthly working time, from 122.7 hours in 1991 to 110.7 hours in 2011,[24] as the number of workers in part-time and atypical forms of employment such as the so-called 'mini-jobs' rose substantially (see Federal Statistical Office, 2009). Even so, a discrepancy is also apparent between hourly labour productivity and hourly wages (see figure 35 (b)). In 2011, hourly wages were only marginally (0.4 per cent) above their 2000 level, while hourly labour productivity had grown by 12.8 per cent over the same period.

Productivity outpaces pay in developed economies

Because some of the larger economies, including the United States, Germany and Japan, have seen wage growth lagging behind productivity growth, our report estimates that in developed economies as a whole average labour productivity has outpaced real average wage growth. Based on the wage data for 36 countries, we estimate that since 1999 average labour productivity has increased more than twice as much as average wages in developed economies (figure 36).

Figure 35 Trends in labour productivity and wages in Germany, 1991–2011: (a) per month; (b) per hour

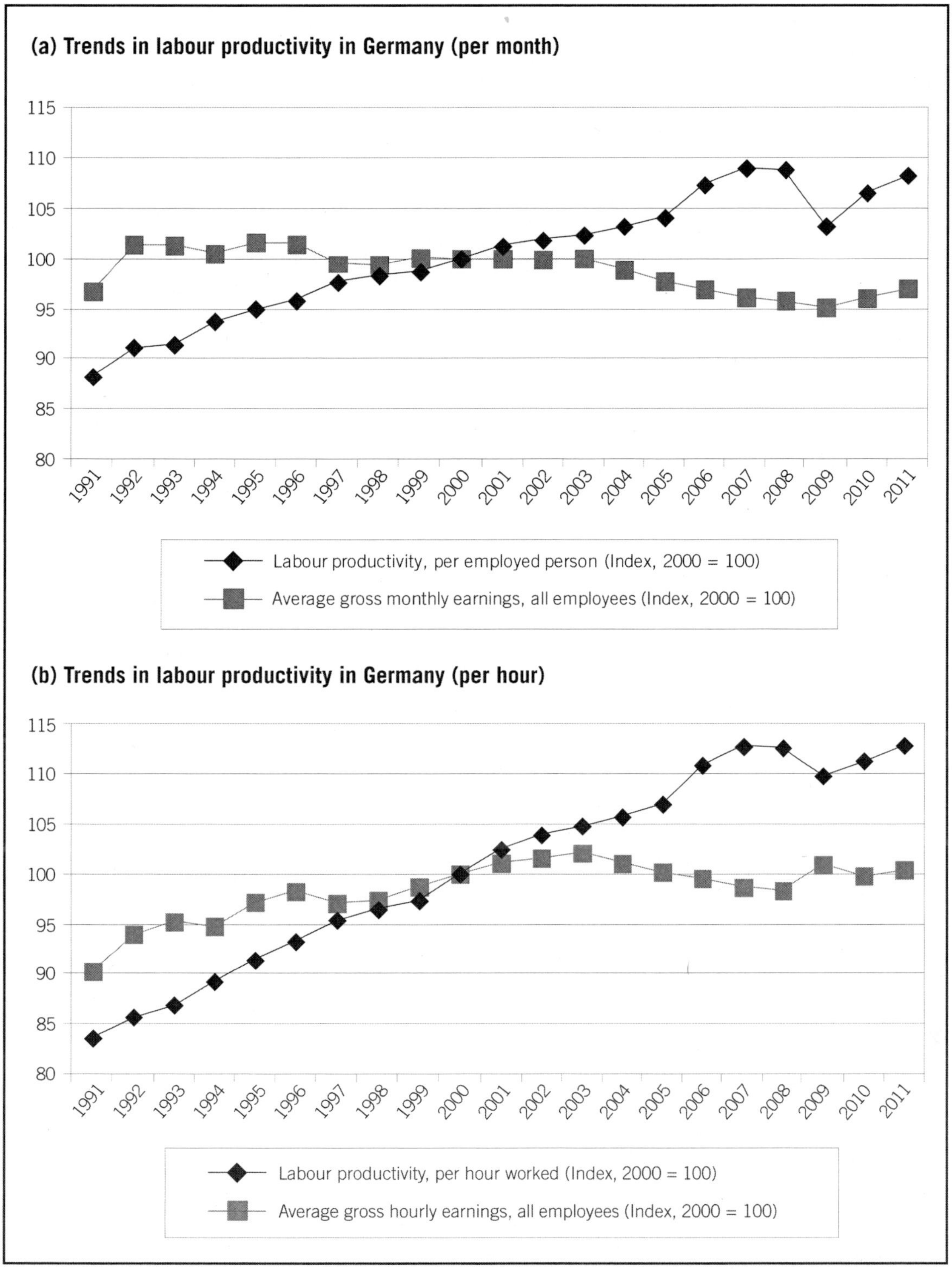

Note: Nominal average monthly and hourly wages published by the Federal Statistical Office have been deflated using the CPI from the same source.

Source: Federal Statistical Office, Germany, National Accounts: Domestic Product, Quarterly Results, Fachserie 18, Series 1.2 (May 2012), table 1.12; Federal Statistical Office, 2012.

Figure 36 Trends in growth in average wages and labour productivity in developed economies (index: 1999 = 100)

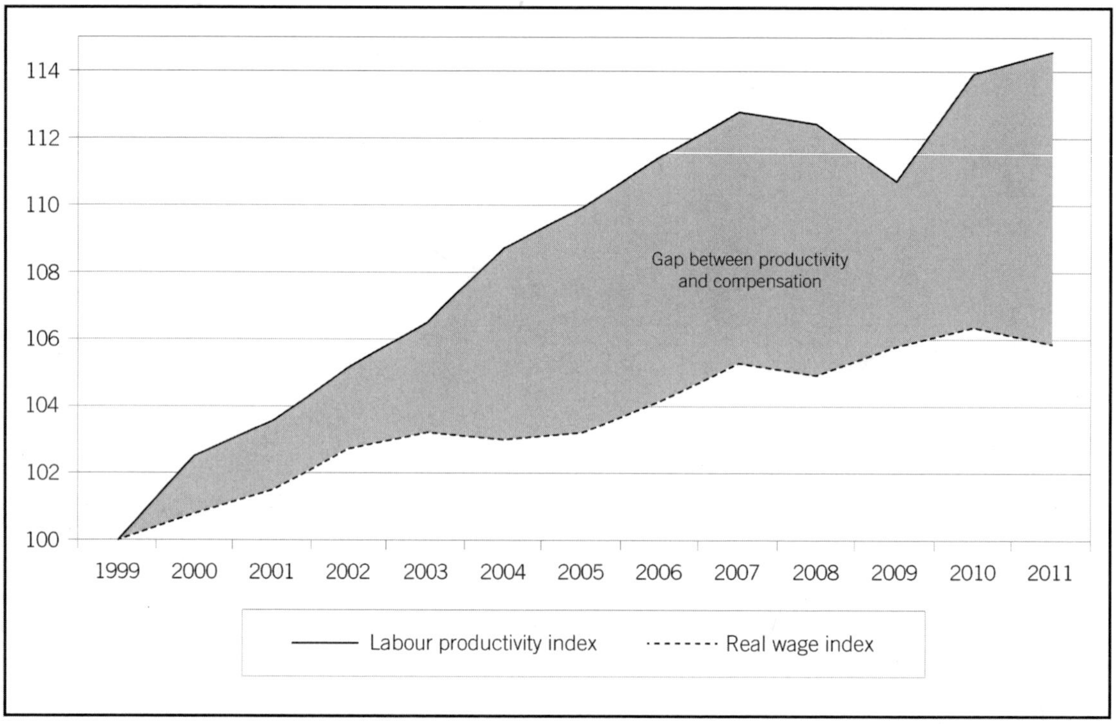

Note: Since the indices refer to a weighted average, developments in the three largest developed economies (United States, Japan and Germany) have a particular impact on this outcome. Labour productivity is measured as output per worker (see note 9).
Sources: ILO Global Wage Database; ILO Trends Econometric Model, March 2012.

5.3 The role of financial markets and other factors

The search for explanations

Most studies that have documented the fall in the labour income share since the 1980s have also tried to understand its causes (see, for example, IMF, 2007; European Commission, 2007; OECD, 2012a; ILO, 2008a; ILO 2010a; IILS, 2012).

The analysis undertaken in the previous *Global Wage Report* explored the possibility that trends in the labour share were determined by a compositional shift in employment from labour-intensive to more capital-intensive sectors, where labour shares are lower. The analysis showed that the shift in sectoral composition was indeed a contributory factor, but that most of the fall in the labour share was the result of falling shares *within industries* (ILO, 2010a). A recent OECD study confirmed this finding, pointing out that "within-industry falls in the labour share explain an overwhelming proportion of its aggregate decrease between 1990 and 2007" (OECD, 2012b, p. 119). Large falls were observed in financial intermediation, and also in high- and medium-technology manufacturing, while the decline was less steep in other service sectors, construction and low-tech manufacturing.

New evidence: Revisiting the "usual suspects"

The present report goes further and provides a new set of empirical evidence. Figure 37 provides an illustration of the "usual suspects": technological change, globalization, financial markets, labour market institutions, and the decline in the bargaining power of labour. In our illustration, the circles for technological change, globalization and financial markets overlap, reflecting the difficulties in distinguishing between these phenomena at both conceptual and empirical levels. The structure of the diagram also indicates that the bargaining power of labour derives directly from labour market institutions (particularly the existence and strength of trade unions) but is also influenced by globalization and financial markets, which give firms more options for investing in financial assets as well as in real assets, both at home and abroad (Rodrik, 1997; Onaran, 2011). In fact, while much evidence has focused on the role of globalization and especially technology, many studies have overlooked the potential effects of financial markets and of the downsizing of labour and social institutions.

Figure 37 Factors influencing the labour income share

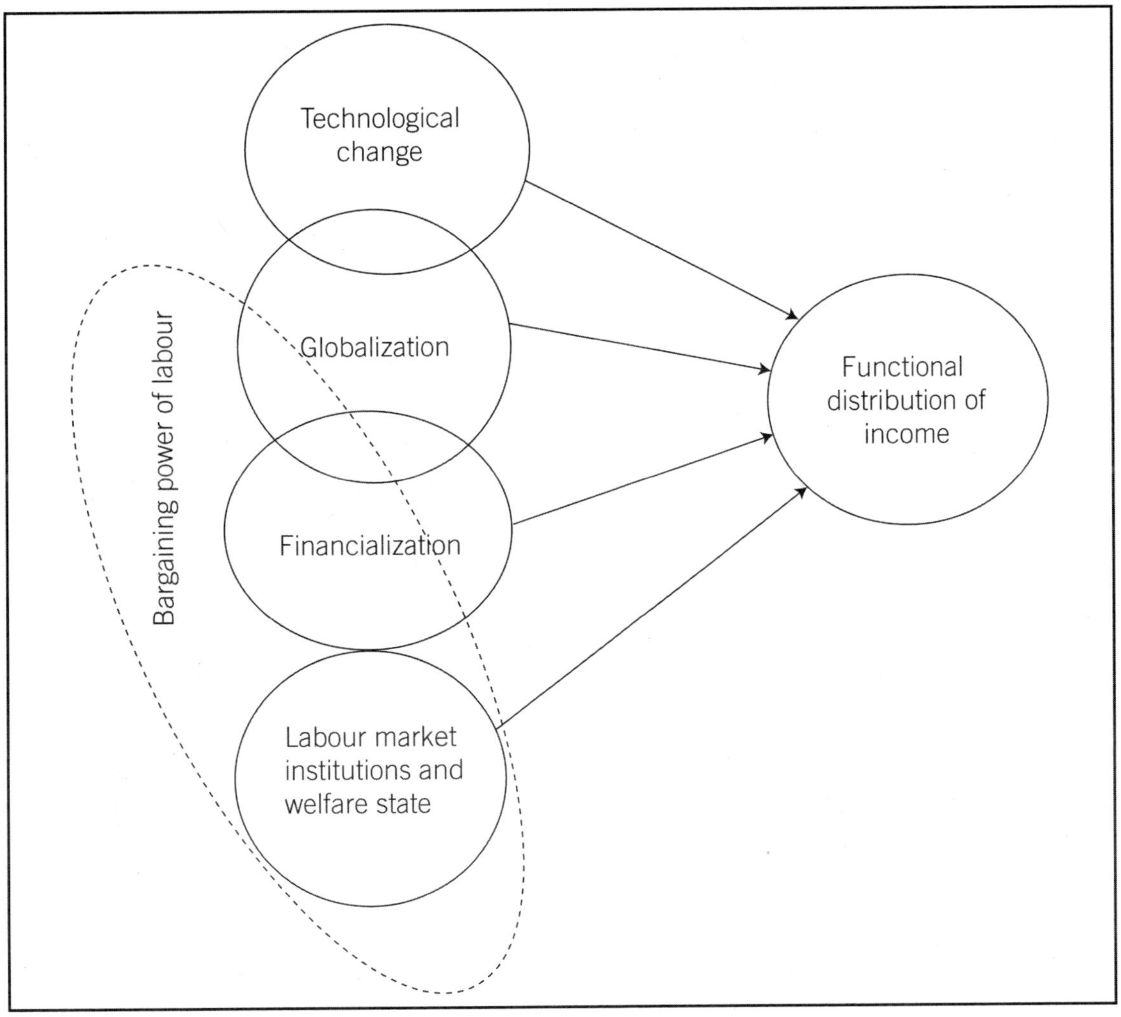

Source: Stockhammer, forthcoming.

Technological changes are often presented as the main culprit, with the suggestion that they have been "capital augmenting" rather than "labour augmenting", increasing the demand for capital and complementary high-skilled labour and reducing the demand for low-skilled workers (see IMF, 2007; European Commission, 2007; OECD, 2012b; IILS, 2012).[25] The standard hypothesis is that the diffusion of information and communication technologies (ICT) has allowed for automation of production, boosting productivity and displacing low-skilled workers. The latest OECD study estimated that technical change and capital accumulation accounted, on average, for 80 per cent of intra-industry change of the labour share in advanced economies over the period 1990–2007 (OECD, 2012b).

Studies typically also find negative but smaller effects of globalization on the labour share. One possible explanation for this is that the intensification of competition and the entry of labour-abundant countries into the global economy may have worked as a wage-moderating factor (ILO, 2008a). More recent firm-level evidence produced in a joint ILO–WTO publication (Bacchetta and Jansen, 2011) shows that increased competition from trade liberalization has often induced firms in both developed and developing countries to become more productive through a process of "industry rationalization", involving the elimination of the least productive firms and the dismissal of workers in the remaining firms. It is also possible that redistribution from labour to capital has occurred through offshoring or the so-called "threat effects" that can occur even without actual changes in production locations (Epstein and Burke, 2001; see also Messenger and Ghosheh, 2010, on service sector offshoring and outsourcing).

A new focus on financialization

The globalization of financial markets and "financialization" – defined as the increasing role of financial motives, financial actors and financial institutions in the operation of domestic and international economies (Epstein, 2005) – have been brought into the picture only more recently. A report by the IILS found that the international integration of financial markets has been a major driver of falling wage shares, at least in advanced economies (IILS, 2011). The switch in the 1980s to corporate governance systems based on maximizing shareholder value and the rise of aggressive returns-oriented institutions, including private equity funds, hedge funds and institutional investors, put pressure on firms to increase profits , especially in the short term (Rossmann, 2009; Lazonick and O'Sullivan, 2000; Stockhammer, 2004; see also IILS, 2008; Hein and Schoder, 2011; Argitis and Pitelis, 2001). In addition, as pointed out above, financial globalization has probably weakened workers' bargaining position (Rodrik, 1997; Onaran, 2011). Some groups of workers, particularly top executives, may have benefited from this process of "financialization" through deferred salaries in the form of pension funds and other types of capital gains. For the average worker, though, the evidence indicates that the extent and size of such gains are much more limited.

Labour market institutions: Declining collective power?

Labour market institutions and the size of the welfare state are also among the variables that have been debated in the existing literature. These institutional indicators include factors such as union density, minimum wage legislation, unemployment benefits and coverage, severance pay, or government consumption. The decline in union density – the number of trade union members as a percentage of total employees or as a percentage of total employment – in many developed economies has often been linked to the weakening of workers' bargaining power, negatively affecting their ability to negotiate a larger share of the pie for labour compensation. The level of the minimum wage and other "intermediary" institutions, including employment protection legislation, the generosity of unemployment benefit and other benefits and contributions (the 'tax wedge'), are among the institutional variables that have been included in empirical studies (IMF, 2007; European Commission, 2007; OECD, 2012b). The level of unemployment benefit can have an impact on the labour share by affecting workers' "reservation wages", that is, the level of pay workers would accept as a minimum.

Deepening the analysis

The estimates in the present report provide new evidence to complement and update existing studies. Our analysis covers a wider range of countries and a longer period of time, drawing on the recently updated ILO Global Wage Database and other complementary data sources.[26] It includes annual data from 71 countries (31 high-income economies and 40 developing economies, including emerging economies) for the period 1970–2007. Although data were available for the years 2007–09, the crisis period was excluded to avoid the effect of structural breaks on the underlying historical trend and because our main interest lies in the long-term trends in the run up to the crisis. The estimates are based on a model that captures the factors in figure 37. Appendix III provides a step-by-step account of the methodology used for estimation and summarizes the main results for the regression outcomes. The countries included are also described in the appendix.

Figure 38 shows the results we obtained by decomposing the effects of the different factors that enter the model to explain changes in labour income shares over time. This decomposition was calculated by weighting the measurable changes between two selected periods (1990/04 and 2000/04) for each of the factors where the weights are the estimated coefficients in the selected model (shown in table A4 of Appendix III). The decompositions are estimated separately for developed and developing economies. Figure 38(a) shows that in the case of developed economies all factors contributed to the fall in the labour income share over time, with global financialization playing the largest role. The estimates mean that, in terms of relative contribution, global financialization contributes 46 per cent of the fall in labour income shares, compared to contributions of 19 per cent by globalization, 10 per cent by technology and 25 per cent by changes in two broad institutional variables: government consumption and union density. These results open up the possibility that the impact of finance may have been underestimated in many of the previous studies and suggest that overlooking the role of financial markets may have serious implications for our understanding of the causes of labour share trends.

The negative contribution of the institutional factors to the labour income share can be explained with reference to the diminution, on average, of government consumption as a share of GDP and union density in advanced economies. In other words, while the positive and significant coefficients of these variables (see table A4) imply that

Figure 38 Decomposing changes in the average adjusted labour income share between 1990–94 and 2000–04

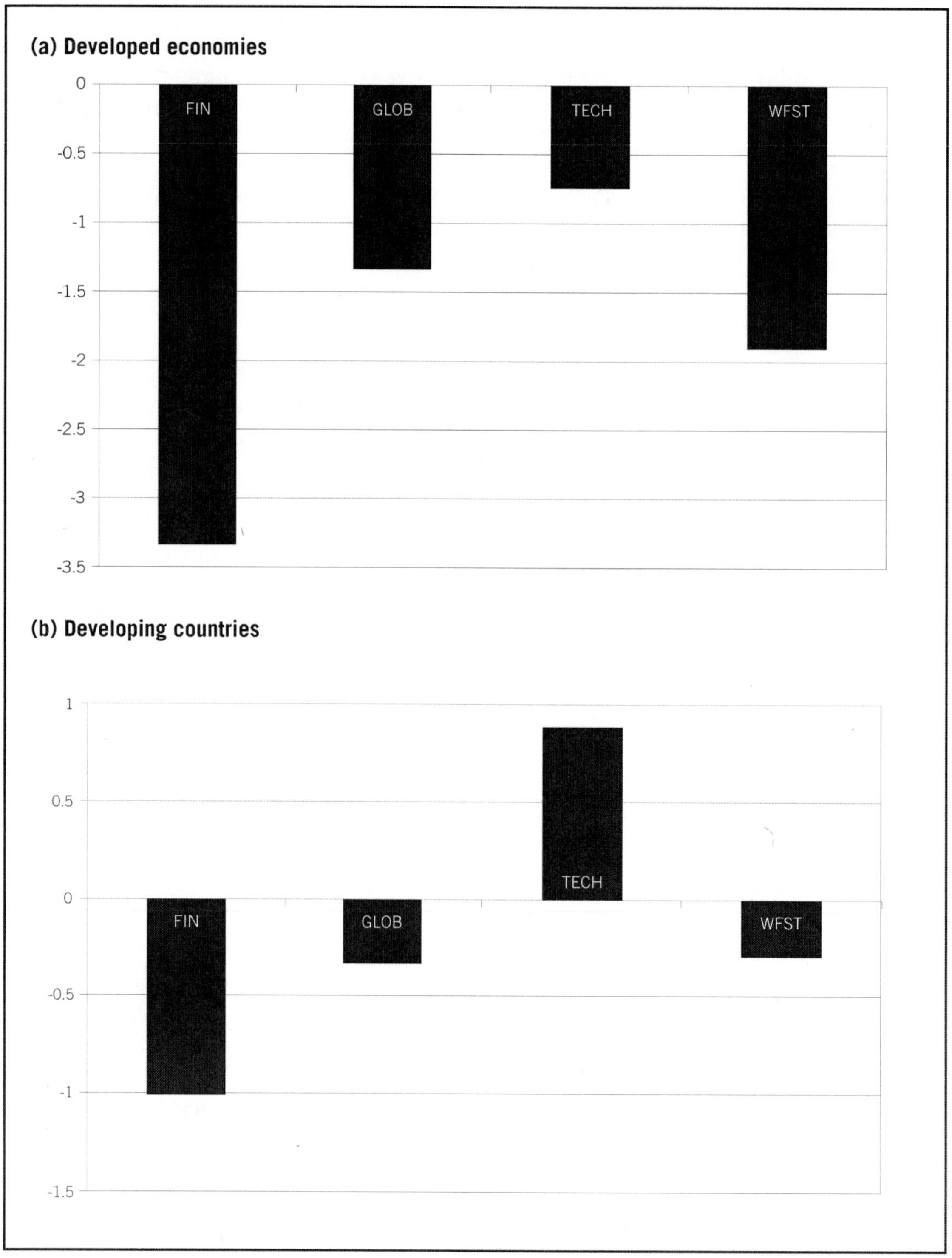

Notes: The decomposition is based on estimates in table A4. (a) Developed economies (table A4, column 3); (b) developing countries (table A4, column 4). FIN stands for "financialization"; GLOB stands for "globalization"; TECH stands for "technology"; WFST stands for "welfare state measures and labour market institutions". See Appendix III for a detailed explanation of the steps leading to the decomposition.

Source: ILO estimates (Stockhammer, forthcoming).

increases in government consumption and union density have a positive impact on labour income shares, the actual drop in both government consumption and unionization has contributed to a decline in the labour share. On the other hand, financialization, globalization and technological progress have all grown in magnitude over time, thus contributing negatively to changes in labour income shares between the two periods.

In the case of developing economies, figure 38(b) illustrates our finding of a positive impact of technology on the labour share, which might possibly be explained by some "catching up" effect of economic growth, with a tightening of labour markets and the draining of excess labour supply. This technology effect partly offsets the adverse effects of financialization, globalization and the shrinkage in the welfare state. Nevertheless, as was the case with the decomposition for developed economies, financialization stands as the single most adverse factor in terms of explaining the decline of labour income shares among the economies in the developing world that are included in our sample.

In addition to these variables, increases in unemployment also have strong negative impacts on the labour share, which should not come as a surprise given the downward pressure on wages and the weakening of workers' bargaining position in the presence of higher rates of unemployment (see Appendix III).

6 The effects of labour income shares on economic growth

6.1 Falling labour shares and aggregate demand: Ambiguous effects

Equity and economics: What happens when the labour share falls?

Because factor shares (capital share and labour share) link income to productive activity, they are often seen as an indicator of the fairness of the distribution of income. Also, as pointed out by Atkinson, factor shares are a crucial issue in collective bargaining, where a fair division of income may be regarded as one where increased labour productivity is reflected in increased labour compensation (Atkinson, 2009). Some commentators also consider that decreasing labour shares may have political consequences.[27]

Analysing the effects on aggregate demand

While these are important considerations, this section of the present report focuses on the economic implications of declining labour shares. In particular, we underline the fact that changes in labour share have different effects on the various key components of the aggregate demand for goods and services produced in an economy. Aggregate demand is the sum of consumption by households, private sector investment, net exports and government consumption. The economic mechanism illustrated in figure 39 indicates that a shift between the two components of the functional income distribution (labour and capital shares) affects the main elements of aggregate demand and ultimately these changes affect national income growth in a dynamic process.

But how exactly does a decline in the labour share affect aggregate demand? This question has so far received relatively less attention, and does not have a simple answer. We have set out to explore empirically the link between the observed changes

Figure 39 The macroeconomic effects of functional income shares

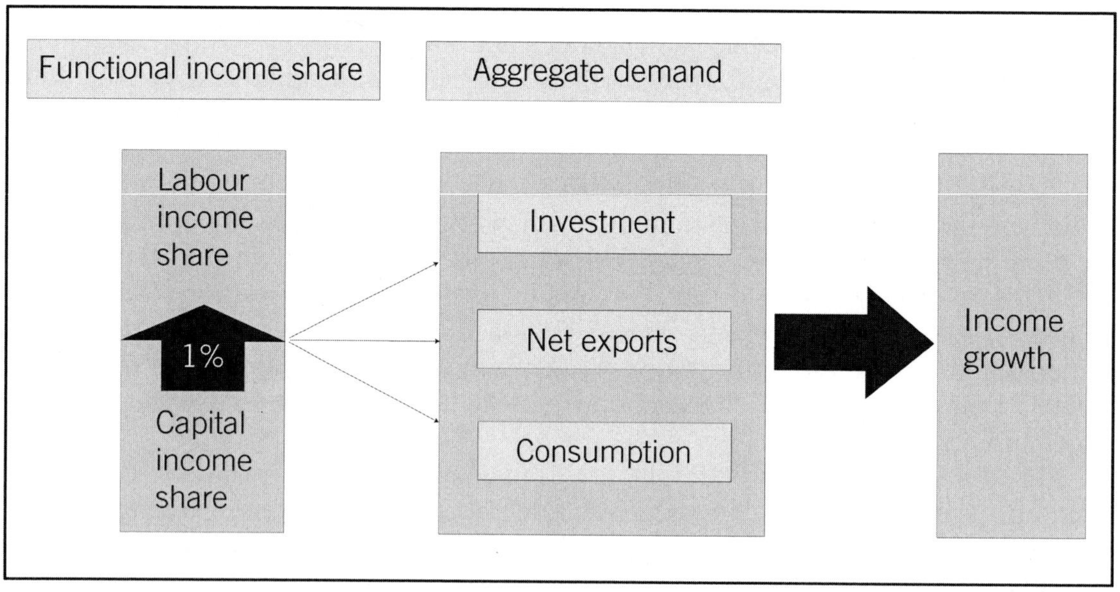

Source: ILO.

in labour income shares in the past four decades (1960s to 2000s) and each of the main components of aggregate demand, namely consumption, investment and net exports.[28] We have restricted our analysis to 15 countries that are members of the G20 and for which sufficient data are available, and also look at the 12 eurozone member countries as a group. The methodology in estimating the effect of wage shares on aggregate demand and detailed results are provided in Appendix IV, and the main direction of results is shown in table 2.[29]

Table 2 Direction of effects of a 1% decrease in labour income share on private consumption of domestic goods and services, investment and net exports in 16 economies

	Private consumption	Investment	Net exports
Eurozone	↘	↗	↗
Argentina	↘	→	↗
Australia	↘	↗	↗
Canada	↘	↗	↗
China	↘	→	↗↗
France	↘	↗	↗
Germany	↘	↗	↗
India	↘	→	↗
Italy	↘	↗	↗
Japan	↘	↗	↗
Mexico	↘	↗	↗
Republic of Korea	↘	→	↗
South Africa	↘	↗	↗
Turkey	↘	→	↗
United Kingdom	↘	↗	↗
United States	↘	→	↗

Source: Onaran and Galanis, forthcoming.

Consumption down, exports up, investment uncertain

The table illustrates the finding that a 1 per cent decline in the labour share has been consistently associated with a lower share of private consumption relative to GDP in all 15 countries, as well as in the eurozone as a whole. Conversely, a 1 per cent lower labour share was associated with a higher share of net exports in all countries, particularly in China (as highlighted by the two upward arrows) which has pursued a highly explicit export-led growth strategy. The link between labour shares and investment is less clear-cut. A 1 per cent lower labour share was associated with higher rates of investment in GDP in nine countries as well as in the eurozone group, but had no perceptible effect on investment in five emergent economies and the United States.

The positive effect of lower labour share on exports is perhaps not surprising, given the close relationship between the concept of the labour share and the concept of unit labour costs (labour costs per unit of output; for more detail on this relationship, see Appendix I). A decline in unit labour costs is often seen as an improvement in external cost competitiveness, particularly in the eurozone, where individual Member States cannot devalue their currency or adjust interest rates, and where lower unit labour costs are therefore frequently advocated as a means of restoring economic growth and promoting employment. This was, for example, the rationale behind the decision in Greece to reduce the minimum wage by 22 per cent, with a further 10 per cent cut for young workers, together with a reduction in non-wage costs (social security contributions) by 5 percentage points (see Part I of this report). Similar, though less radical, measures were also part of IMF programmes in Portugal, Serbia and Latvia.[30]

Private consumption and the labour/capital share

However, a single-minded focus on lowering unit labour costs would fail to take into consideration the generally negative impact of lower wages on private household consumption, and hence the uncertain effect on overall aggregate demand. The positive effect on consumption of redistribution from the capital to the labour share most likely arises because the propensity to consume out of labour compensation is higher than the propensity to consume out of capital income, as the latter is mainly redistributed through dividends to wealthier people who save a higher proportion of their total incomes. It is important to realize, though, that a substantial part of profit accrues to companies, who pass on only a part of it in dividends, and whose retained earnings contribute to generating future labour incomes. Also, a sizeable fraction of the dividends accrues to pension funds, which may pay out pensions at a later date that will be spent on consumption. Furthermore, the State levies taxes on capital income and pays transfers that may be an important determinant of consumption. Nevertheless, in spite of these complexities, we find that labour compensation and household consumption remain positively correlated.

Investment: Resources for the "real economy"

The relationship between the labour share and investment is less clear. In principle one could expect that higher capital incomes might lead to more productive investment, and this indeed seems to have been the case in a majority of countries. But there are also concerns that financialization may have drained internal means of finance for real investment purposes away from corporations, through increases in dividend payments in order to boost stock prices and thus shareholder value, or through risky financial investments aimed at generating maximum short-run profits. Both types of activity may have had negative effects on investment in capital stock in the "real economy".[31] In emerging economies, one possible explanation for the lack of correlation between firms' profits and overall investment may lie in the dominance of public industrial policies and public investment as the drivers of infrastructure and industrial development (Akyuz et al., 1998). This hypothesis, though, calls for further research.

The labour share and aggregate demand: A delicate balance

Overall, our findings highlight the ambiguous effects that changes in the labour income share can have on aggregate demand and income growth. In some countries and under some circumstances, low wage growth relative to productivity growth might lead to increases in net exports, in domestic capital investment, and in income growth.[32] In other countries or other circumstances, low wage growth and a falling labour share might depress domestic consumption to such an extent that any gains in net exports and/or investment could not offset an overall drop in aggregate demand and income growth. That both outcomes are possible, however, indicates that changes in the functional distribution of national income between labour and capital do have an unpredictable impact on a country's overall economic performance. This observation renders it imperative that decision-makers continuously monitor the evolution of wages in relation to productivity and study the effects on national income. But a presumption that wage moderation is always beneficial for economic activity would be misguided.

6.2 In pursuit of the optimal labour share

National and global strategies

This uncertainty about the effects of functional income shares on economic growth raises the question of what the net effect is of a change in a country's labour share. This net effect certainly varies from country to country and is also likely to vary over time, depending on internal and external circumstances. In some countries and some periods, a redistribution of income from capital to labour will provide a boost to national income, while in other countries and at other times it will have the opposite effect. The net effect of a changing labour income share in any given country will necessarily depend on the international environment and on the strategies that are being pursued in all other countries at that moment.

Export-driven growth

In recent years, many countries have pursued export-led growth strategies based on low unit labour costs. Strong types of "export-driven" growth were observed in China and Germany, but also to a greater or lesser extent in Argentina, Canada, Japan, Indonesia, the Republic of Korea and Russia. Over the years 2000–08, all these countries maintained trade surpluses. In China, the large export surplus alone guaranteed an average

Figure 40 Unit labour costs in selected eurozone countries, 2000–10 (index: 2000 = 100)

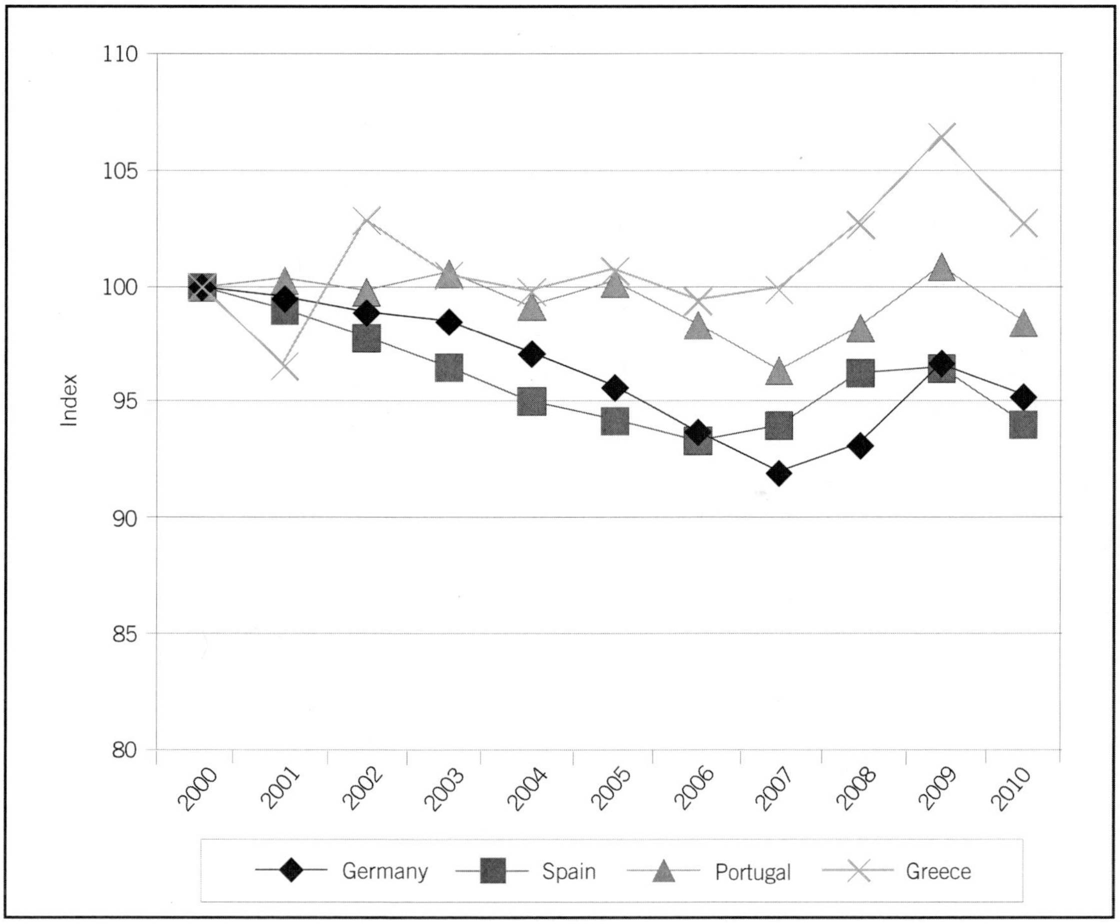

Source: Calculated from Eurostat. Real unit labour cost is defined as compensation per employee in current prices divided by GDP in current prices per employed person.

rate of economic growth in excess of 2.5 per cent per year, and accounted for about one-quarter of overall economic growth (reflecting the extraordinary rates of expansion of both private household consumption and, especially, investment). In the case of Germany, where annual growth rates were much lower, private consumption barely increased at all and the export surplus accounted for between one-third and one-half of economic expansion. China's export growth was based on a particularly competitive exchange rate. In Germany – a eurozone member that cannot devalue its currency unilaterally – export surpluses were boosted by low inflation and falling real unit labour costs relative to other eurozone countries (figure 40).

Debt-driven growth

Because one country's surplus is another country's deficit, not all countries can follow the path of China and Germany. Export-driven growth requires high current account surpluses in some countries and thus deficits in others. In some of the world's main "demand engines" consumption booms since the turn of the century were underpinned by soaring household debt rather than by rising wages. In the United States in particular, strong consumption growth in the face of stagnating median wages was made possible only by wealth-based and debt-financed consumption. Stock market and housing price booms have each increased (notional) wealth and thus collateral for consumer credit and mortgage financed consumption.[33] In addition, changing financial norms, new financial instruments (credit card debt, home equity lending) and deterioration of creditworthiness standards, triggered by the securitization of mortgage debt, made increasing amounts of credit available to low-income, low-wealth households, in particular. Household debt thus became a substitute for higher wages as a source of demand and consumption.

This debt-driven growth sustained global economic growth in the years before the crisis. Had falling labour shares of the bottom 99 per cent in the United States not been compensated for by debt-led consumption, it is likely that world economic growth would have slowed or halted much earlier. Debt-driven consumption booms can be observed not only in the United States, but also to a greater or lesser extent in the United Kingdom, Australia, and the so-called "rescue economies" in the eurozone (Greece, Ireland, Portugal and Spain). Figure 41 shows that current account deficits are associated with higher household debt for a selection of advanced economies that have in common easy access to credit markets, indicative of how finacialization has contributed to external imbalances by channelling resources into household debt for consumption demand.

Demand-led growth

Other countries follow more balanced models of 'demand-led' growth, based on wages increasing in line with productivity rather than on household debt. In France (as in the United States and the United Kingdom), growth was driven by domestic demand. Net wealth–income ratios and residential property prices also increased. Yet in France, unlike in the United States and the United Kingdom, domestic demand was almost entirely based on wages increasing in line with productivity, rather than on debt-financed consumption demand. The ratio of gross household debt to income increased only slightly and the financial balance of the private household sector remained positive, as did the financial balance of the private sector as a whole. Among the emerging economies, Brazil perhaps stands out, with increases both in the labour share and in the contribution of domestic demand to real GDP growth.

Yet even in Brazil there are signs of debt-driven consumption, on top of wage-based consumption (Bruno, 2011). The reason for this is that in Brazil the average wage earner has a very high propensity to consume: studies find that most wage earners spend 100 per cent of their salaries, with private savings deriving solely from profits made by the upper percentiles in the personal income distribution. At the same time, through the impact of financialization, Brazil has experienced an expansion in lending and reduced the average propensity to save of the average household. This has been particularly fuelled by lower interest rates maintained by the authorities to encourage investment. Although such an environment benefits those who promote capital investment, it is also leading to an accumulation of debt that fuels economic growth through consumption.

Figure 41 Changes in current account balance and household debt in selected countries, 2003–10

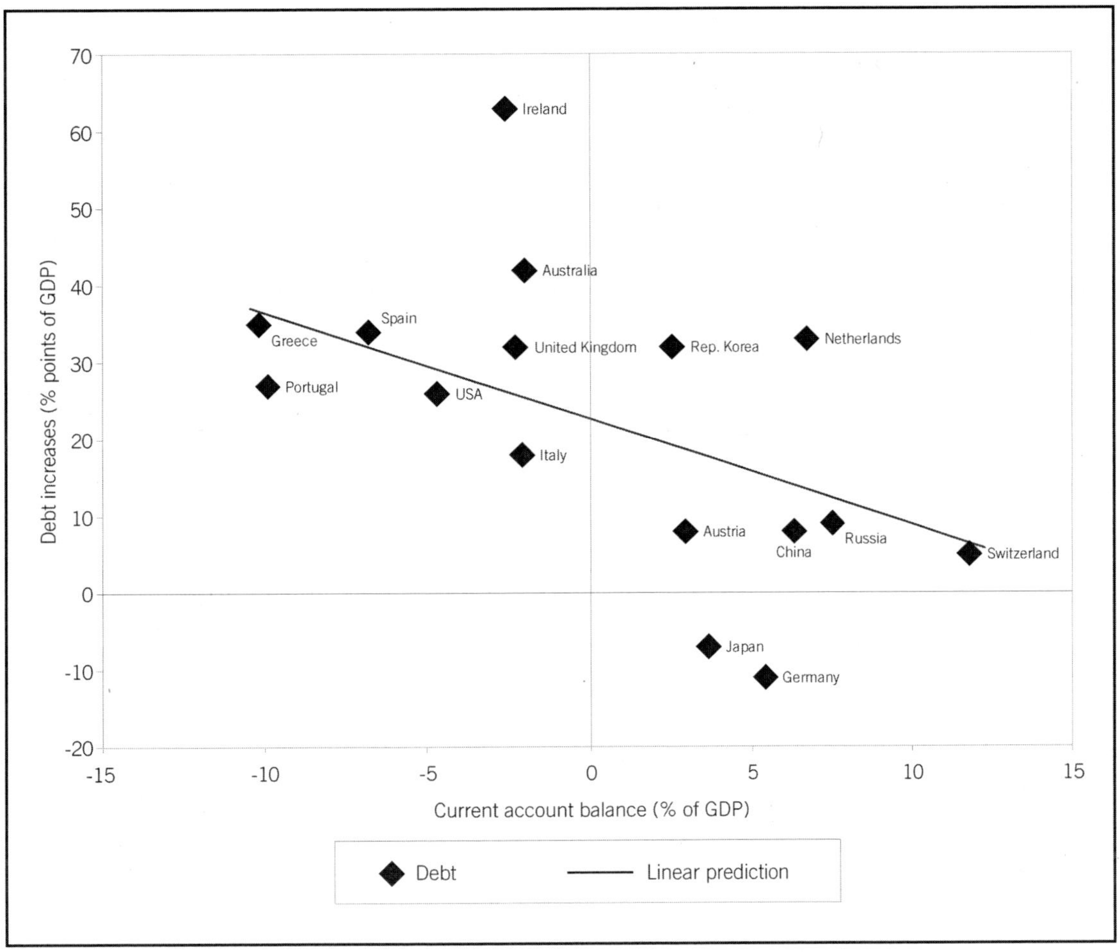

Notes: Current account balances are given as averages for the period 2003–10. Increases in household debt are given as averages between 2000 and 2008. Ireland starts at 2001; Switzerland starts at 1999 and ends in 2007. The line in the scatter diagram is based on only 16 observations, which may not be sufficient to generate a statistically reliable estimate.
Source: Created from Lavoie and Stockhammer, forthcoming, table 13.

6.3 The "Great Recession" and the opportunity for more balanced growth

The different growth patterns described above can work for some countries for some time, but recent experience has shown that debt-driven consumption was not sustainable at either the national or the global level. Debt-driven growth comes with rising levels of household debt and excesses in pay and risk-taking in the financial sector. The crisis and its subsequent painful deleveraging process have revealed the limits of this growth model, which not only rested on internal imbalances, but also contributed to global imbalances as high (or rising) current account surpluses in some countries required the existence of deficits in others.

Managing competition in a closed global economy

What is the way forward? In many cases, the policy advice to those economies that had large current account deficits and household debts prior to the crisis involved some combination of austerity and wage moderation (or wage cuts) to increase net exports. This advice is based on the assumption that a unilateral downward adjustment in labour costs can restore individual countries' competitiveness. The extent to which this can work is unclear, as competitiveness not only depends on labour costs but also on a series of other factors, including the ability of countries to produce a wide range of diverse and complex products (Felipe and Kumar, 2011). There is also a problem of collective action: while each individual country may in principle increase aggregate demand for its goods and services by exporting more, not all countries can do so at the same time. The world economy as a whole is a closed economy. If competitive wage cuts or wage moderation policies are pursued simultaneously in a large number of countries, competitive gains will cancel out and the regressive effect of global wage cuts on consumption could lead to a worldwide depression of aggregate demand. There is also room to stimulate domestic demand in countries with a current account surplus.

Moreover, the advice to cut unit labour costs seems to be based on the consensus that surplus economies are the result of successful export-led strategies whereas debt-led growth economies have lost competitiveness in their market for exports and, as result, have relied on consumption fuelled by debt. It is indeed true that countries such as Greece and Spain have experienced increasing current account deficits. It is striking, however, that this happened in spite of increases in the real value of their exports. What led to the deterioration in these countries' current accounts was the significant increase in imports between 2003 and 2008 and the negative impact of the so-called "factor income" of the current account: that is, servicing loans from and credits to foreign investors. Further cuts to unit labour costs are unlikely to solve the latter part of the current account deficit.

PART III | Implications for equitable growth

7 Internal and external imbalances

The *Global Wage Report* is a contribution to a wider literature on the changes in the distribution and levels of wages within and across countries, as well as on the economic and social implications of these trends. Some stylized facts emerge from this literature. One of the key findings is the downward trend in the labour share and the growing inequality in personal income distribution.

7.1 Functional and personal income distribution

A smaller share for workers

In terms of functional income distribution, which concerns how national income has been distributed between labour and capital, the present report has shown that there is a long-term trend towards a falling share of labour compensation and a rising share of profits in many countries. This confirms the findings of the *Global Wage Report 2010/11* (2010a), which identified a declining trend in the labour share in 17 out of 24 developed economies since the 1980s, and of the OECD's *Employment Outlook 2012* (2012b) which described a similar trend in 26 out of 30 countries since 1990. This indicates that there have been discrepancies between wages and labour productivity growth in a large number of countries.

A growing gap between top and bottom earners

The personal distribution of wages has also become more unequal. The distance between the top 10 per cent and the bottom 10 per cent of wage earners has increased in 23 out of 31 countries since 1995–97 (ILO, 2008a), and the proportion of those with low pay (defined as less than two-thirds of the median wage) has also increased in 25 out of 37 countries (ILO, 2010a). Such trends towards growing inequality remain strong when other income sources, taxation, and income transfer are considered.

7.2 Wage-based consumption is down, affecting the recovery

These internal imbalances have tended to create or exacerbate external imbalances. The skewed distribution in favour of capital income has tended to suppress consumption demand. In some countries, consumption kept growing mostly as a result of a phenomenal increase in household debts. Other countries have looked for solutions outside, with export surpluses compensating for weak domestic demand. But, ultimately, relying on easy credit turned out to be unsustainable, and export-led growth strategies based on trade surpluses were also often only possible in combination with the debt-driven consumption in deficit countries.

These imbalances all appeared before the Great Recession. While the full impact of the crisis on these external and internal imbalances is not yet clear, there are few reasons for excessive optimism. Average wages have declined in developed economies in 2008 and 2011. Cuts in labour costs in crisis countries with current account deficits involve economic risks: unless surplus countries allow for more wage-based consumption on both domestic and imported goods, the result could be a protracted period of economic stagnation, or even recession.

The risks of austerity and recession

As for internal imbalances, austerity policies and a prolonged period of economic downturn are unlikely to reverse trends in the personal distribution of wages and incomes. Although the labour share briefly bounced back at the beginning of the crisis it began to decline again after 2009. At the same time there are indications that the crisis may have further increased inequality. In the United States the increase in income inequality between 2010 and 2011 was the largest on record since 1993 and the number of "working poor" has now reached 7.2 per cent of all workers in 2011, up from 5.7 per cent in 2007 (US Census Bureau, various years). In Europe, over 8 per cent of people with a job are at risk of poverty and can be qualified as "working poor" according to the European Commission's *Employment and Social Developments in Europe 2011* (2012c).

These developments not only have consequences on economic stability and growth, but they also challenged the notion of social justice and undermine social cohesion. Unequal distribution and concentration of incomes among top earners and the owners of capital have been the cause of public dissatisfaction across the world, increasing the risk of social unrest and social instability. In developed economies, they have reduced the acceptance of austerity and fiscal consolidation measures. In developing countries, they have sparked a multitude of strikes and protests, especially when food and energy price increases have simultaneously eroded the purchasing power of wage earners at the bottom.

8 Reconnecting wages and productivity

8.1 Coordinated policy action

What should be done? Our analysis suggests that policy actions towards "rebalancing" should be taken at both national and global levels. In doing so, a simplistic view that countries can just "cut" their way out of the recession needs to be avoided, and more emphasis should be placed on policies that promote a close connection between the growth of labour productivity and the growth of workers' compensation. The existence of a large current-account surplus in some countries indicates that there is room to stimulate domestic demand, notably by better linking wage and productivity increases. Great care should be taken not to promote a "race to the bottom" in labour shares in deficit countries or throughout the Eurozone. Unrestrained pursuit of labour cost advantage in securing economic competitiveness is likely to discourage economic innovation and upgrading which have constituted key dynamics of the market economy. Austerity measures that are imposed from the outside, bypassing social partners, will also harm effective labour relations. Thus, global-level policy coordination which can prevent the "low-road" option is strongly recommended to create favourable environments for "internal rebalancing".

8.2 Strengthening existing institutions

"Internal rebalancing" can begin by strengthening institutions for wage determination. This report highlights that the weakening of such institutions and hence workers' bargaining position has contributed to the deterioration in both functional and personal income distribution. Thus, policies are needed to "rebalance" bargaining power for economic efficiency and social stability. Given the difficulty with organizing workers, particularly in the context of increasing labour market segmentation and rapid technological changes, more supporting and enabling environments need to be created for collective bargaining and to enable workers to demand a fair share of economic output. At the same time, it should be noted that these workers, particularly low-paid workers, have shouldered a greater burden of the widening inequality and need more protection when it comes to wage determination. Minimum wages, if properly designed, have proved an effective policy tool which can provide a decent wage floor and thus secure a minimum living standard for these workers and their families. As the latest *World Development Report 2013: Jobs* (World Bank, 2012) has shown, the potential negative impacts of collective bargaining arrangements and minimum wages on employment and other labour market outcomes have been rather over-stated in the past, while some care needs to be taken in designing them to improve their effectiveness.

8.3 Beyond labour markets

Financial regulation

The findings of our report make it clear that it will not be enough to "rebalance" income redistribution solely through labour market policies. As others have indicated (OECD, 2011 and 2012a; IILS, 2011 and 2012), one important contributing factor to the widening inequality is the policies that have led to unconstrained "financial globalization". Financialization has created incentives for diverting corporations' internal means of finance from real investment into risky speculative financial investments aimed at generating maximum short-run profits. Unregulated financial markets have not only exacerbated inequality but also tended to produce suboptimal and unstable economic outcomes. Therefore, "rebalancing" requires better regulation of the financial sector and restoring their role in channelling resources into productive and sustainable investments.

Taxation and social security

There are other critical dimensions of "rebalancing" which deserve a more detailed analysis. Taxation, the subject of intense debates, is one of them. In various countries, the current taxation scheme tends to be relatively generous to capital incomes when compared to labour incomes, which increases pressure on both labour costs to employers and the take-home pay of workers. Another important area which deserves emphasis is social security and income policies. Our analysis of the labour income share indicates that changes in social security system have impacts not just on income redistribution but also on the primary income distribution such as the labour share. The latter can take place in various channels, including by weakening workers' bargaining position through reducing their fall-back position (e.g. unemployment benefits) or what economists call "reservation wages". Therefore, adequate social security benefits can contribute to creating more favorable institutional environments for effective wage bargaining and to secure basic income for workers in need. At the same time, it is essential that a balance is found between the costs and benefits of social security systems for society and different groups of financers and beneficiaries.

8.4 Specificities of developing countries

The above policies apply to both developed and developing countries. The latter group of countries however faces some specific challenges.

Reaching other earners

First, it must be recognized that only about half of all workers in developing and emerging countries are wage earners – most of the others are self-employed or family helpers. This does not mean that minimum wages and collective bargaining are irrelevant. This report has shown that in a sample of 32 developing countries taken at different points in time in the period 1997–2006 no less than 64 million wage workers were earning less than PPP$2 per day. Minimum wages and collective bargaining can be ways for these workers and their families to achieve higher living standards. But additional measures are needed to create more wage jobs and to raise the productivity and earnings of those in self-employment. Employment guarantee schemes that pay minimum wages are also ways to create incentives for private firms to comply with the minimum wage in order not to lose their workforce.

Improving labour productivity

Additionally, wages are generally much lower in developing and emerging countries, with average wages – even though increasing faster than in developed economies – typically ranging from anywhere between PPP$150 and PPP$1,000 per month. In this context, raising average labour productivity remains a key challenge which must involve efforts to raise the level of education and the capabilities that are required for productive transformation and economic development, combined with a policy environment that is conducive to growth and job creation.

Implementing social protection schemes

Finally, a key challenge for developing and emerging economies is the development of well-designed social protection systems. These will allow workers and their families to invest in the education of their children, to reduce the amounts of precautionary savings and to develop middle-class consumption patterns. The ILO has shown that effective social protection floors are not beyond what countries can afford, whatever their level of economic development (ILO, 2010e).

Appendix I

Global wage trends: Methodological issues

The methodology used to estimate global and regional wage trends was developed by the ILO's Conditions of Work and Employment Programme (TRAVAIL) for the previous *Global Wage Report* (2010) in collaboration with the Department of Statistics, following proposals formulated by an ILO consultant and three peer reviews made by four independent experts.[34] This appendix describes the methodology adopted as a result of this process.

Concepts and definitions

According to the international classification of status in employment (ICSE-93), "employees" are workers who hold "paid employment jobs", i.e. jobs in which the basic remuneration is not directly dependent on the revenue of the employer. Employees include regular employees, workers in short-term employment, casual workers, outworkers, seasonal workers and other categories of workers holding paid employment jobs.[35]

The word "wage" refers to total gross remuneration, including regular bonuses received by employees during a specified period of time for time worked as well as time not worked, such as paid annual leave and paid sick leave. Essentially, it corresponds to the concept of "total cash remuneration", which is the major component of income related to paid employment.[36] It excludes employers' social security contributions.

"Wages", in the present context, refer to real average monthly wages of employees. Wherever possible, we collected data that refer to all employees (rather than to a subset, such as employees in manufacturing or full-time employees).[37] To adjust for the influence of price changes over different time periods, wages are measured in real terms, i.e. the nominal wage data are adjusted for consumer price inflation in the respective country.[38] Real wage growth refers to the year-on-year change in real average monthly wages of all employees.

Census approach

The methodology used for the global and regional estimates is a census method with non-response. In the census approach, the objective is to find wage data for all countries and to develop an explicit treatment in the case of total non-response (see "Treatment of total non-response", below). We have tried to collect wage data for a total of 177 countries and territories, grouped into six separate regions.[39]

Table A1 Regional groups

Regions	Countries and territories (with abbreviations in parentheses)
Developed economies	Australia (AUS), Austria (AUT), Belgium (BEL), Bulgaria (BUL), Canada (CAN), Cyprus (CYP), Czech Republic (CZR), Denmark (DNK), Estonia (EST), Finland (FIN), France (FRA), Germany (DEU), Greece (GRE), Hungary (HUN), Iceland (ICE), Ireland (IRE), Israel (ISR), Italy (ITA), Japan (JAP), Latvia (LAT), Lithuania (LIT), Luxembourg (LUX), Malta (MTA), Netherlands (NET), New Zealand (NZ), Norway (NOR), Poland (POL), Portugal (POR), Romania (ROM), Slovakia (SVK), Slovenia (SVE), Spain (ESP), Sweden (SWE), Switzerland (CH), United Kingdom (UK), United States (USA)
Eastern Europe and Central Asia	Albania (ALB), Armenia (ARM), Azerbaijan (AZB), Belarus (BLS), Bosnia and Herzegovina (BOS), Croatia (CRO), Georgia (GEO), Kazakhstan (KAZ), Kyrgyzstan Republic (KYR), Republic of Moldova (MOL), Russian Federation (RUS), Serbia (SBA), Tajikistan (TAJ), The Former Yugoslav Republic of Macedonia (FYR), Turkey (TKY), Turkmenistan (TUR), Ukraine (UKR), Uzbekistan (UZB)
Asia	Afghanistan (AFG), Bangladesh (BAN), Bhutan BHU), Brunei Darussalam (BRU), Cambodia (CDA), China (CHI), Fiji (FIJ), Hong Kong (China) (HK), India (IND), Indonesia (ISA), Islamic Republic of Iran (IRA), Korea (North) (NK), Republic of Korea (KOR), Lao People's Democratic Republic (LAO), Macau (China) (MAC), Malaysia (MYA), Republic of Maldives (MDS), Mongolia (MON), Myanmar (MYN), Nepal (NEP), Pakistan (PAK), Papua New Guinea (PAP), Philippines (PHL), Singapore (SNG), Solomon Islands (SOL), Sri Lanka (SRI), Thailand (THA), Timor-Leste (TL), Viet Nam (VN)
Latin America and the Caribbean	Argentina (ARG), Bahamas (The) (BAH), Barbados (BBO), Belize (BZE), Plurinational State of Bolivia (BOL), Brazil (BRA), Chile (CHE), Colombia (COL), Costa Rica (COS), Cuba (CUB), Dominican Republic (DOM), Ecuador (ECU), El Salvador (ELS), Guadeloupe (GDP), Guatemala (GUA), Guyana (GUY), Haiti (HAI), Honduras (HON), Jamaica (JAM), Martinique (MAR), Mexico (MEX), Netherlands Antilles (NAN), Nicaragua (NIC), Panama (PAN), Paraguay (PAR), Peru (PER), Puerto Rico (PR), Suriname (SUR), Trinidad and Tobago (TT), Uruguay (URU), Bolivarian Republic of Venezuela (VZA)
Middle East	Bahrain (BAR), Iraq (IRQ), Jordan (JOR), Kuwait (KUW), Lebanon (LEB), Oman (OMA), Qatar (QAT), Saudi Arabia (SAU), Syrian Arab Republic (SYR), United Arab Emirates (UAE), West Bank and Gaza (WBG), Yemen (YEM)
Africa	Algeria (ALG), Angola (ANG), Benin (BEN), Botswana (BOT), Burkina Faso (BKF), Burundi (BUR), Cameroon (CAM), Cape Verde (CAV), Central African Republic (CAR), Chad (CHA), Comoros (COM), Congo (CON), Côte d'Ivoire (COI), Democratic Republic of the Congo (DRC), Egypt (EGY), Equatorial Guinea (EQG), Eritrea (ERI), Ethiopia (ETH), Gabon (GAB), Gambia (GAM), Ghana (GHA), Guinea (GUI), Guinea-Bissau (GUB), Kenya (KEN), Lesotho (LES), Liberia (LIB), Libya (LBY), Madagascar (MAD), Malawi (MAW), Mali (MAL), Mauritania (MAI), Mauritius (MUS), Morocco (MOR), Mozambique (MOZ), Namibia (NAM), Niger (NIG), Nigeria (NIR), Reunion (REU), Rwanda (RWA), Senegal (SEN), Sierra Leone (SL), Somalia (SOM), South Africa (SA), Sudan (SUD), Swaziland (SWA), United Republic of Tanzania (TAN), Togo (TOG), Tunisia (TUN), Uganda (UGA), Zambia (ZAM), Zimbabwe (ZIM)

To enable easier comparison with regional employment trends, our regional groupings are now compatible with those used in the ILO's Global Employment Trends (GET) model (see table A1). However, we have collapsed several GET regions into a single region for Asia and the Pacific (which includes the GET regions East Asia, South-East Asia and the Pacific, and South Asia) and also for Africa (which comprises North Africa and sub-Saharan Africa). Note that the Republic of Korea and Singapore are now grouped with Asia (and no longer with the advanced countries) and that all 27 member countries of the EU are included under "developed economies". Further, the division between "Central and Eastern Europe" and "Eastern Europe and Central Asia" is no longer maintained, with all former transition countries (apart from members of the EU) and Turkey included in a single grouping, "Eastern Europe and Central Asia". For these regions, the regrouping means that regional wage trends published in the current *Global Wage Report* cannot be directly compared to figures in the previous edition. There have been no changes to the regions Latin America and the Caribbean, or the Middle East. However, some data revisions by national statistical offices mean that regional wage trends have been updated since publication of the last edition. Overall, we succeeded in obtaining wage data from 124 countries and territories, with regional coverage indicated in table A2. We have data from all developed economies and all countries in Eastern Europe and Central Asia. In other regions, although repeated attempts were made to obtain wage figures from national statistical offices and/or international repositories, in some instances wage data were not available. The coverage for the remaining regions ranges from 41.2 per cent (Africa) to 75.0 per cent (Middle East). However, since the database includes wage data for the largest and more prosperous countries, the coverage in terms of employees and the total wage bill is higher than the simple count of countries would suggest. In total, our database contains information for 94.3 per cent of the world's employees who together account for approximately 97.7 per cent of the world's wage bill.

Table A2 Coverage of the Global Wage Database, 2010 (%)

Regional group	Country coverage	Employee coverage	Approximate coverage of total wages
Africa	41.2	59.5	79.3
Asia	69.0	98.3	99.3
Eastern Europe and Central Asia	100.0	100.0	100.0
Developed economies	100.0	100.0	100.0
Latin America and the Caribbean	64.5	85.3	83.9
Middle East	75.0	76.4	91.3
World	70.1	94.3	97.7

Note: Country coverage refers to the number of countries for which we found wage data as a percentage of all the countries in the region, while employee coverage refers to the number of employees in countries with data available as a percentage of all employees in the region (as of 2010). The approximate coverage of total wages is estimated based on the assumption that wage levels vary across countries in line with labour productivity (i.e. GDP per person employed, as of 2010), expressed in 2005 PPP$.

Treatment of item non-response

In some countries for which we found data, the statistical series were incomplete, in the sense that data for some years were missing. Table A3 provides coverage information for each year from 2006 to 2011. As expected, the coverage of the database becomes lower for the most recent years since some statistical offices are still processing these data (most notably China, where wage data for 2011 are not yet available). As a consequence, for 2011 we have real observations for only about 74.5 per cent of the world's total wages, compared to 94.3 per cent in 2010.

While the coverage in the most recent year is good in the developed economies and in Eastern Europe and Central Asia, we have too few real observations for the Middle East in 2010 and 2011 to make a reliable estimate, and therefore the most recent wages trends for the Middle East are likely to change. We also flag regional growth rates as "provisional estimates" when they are based on coverage of *c*. 75 per cent and as "tentative estimates" when the underlying coverage of our database is between 40 and 74 per cent to draw attention to fact that they might be revised once more data become available.

Table A3 Coverage of the Global Wage Database, 2006–11 (%)

Regional group	2006	2007	2008	2009	2010	2011
Africa	79.6	78.1	65.2**	64.8**	64.9**	43.2**
Asia	95.8	96.0	96.2	96.4	96.5	(38.1)
Eastern Europe and Central Asia	98.4	99.0	98.9	98.7	98.6	97.2
Developed economies	100.0	99.2	100.0	99.2	99.4	86.7
Latin America and the Caribbean	84.9	84.7	84.4	84.0	82.6	79.0
Middle East	91.7	91.9	91.7	68.0**	(22.4)	(12.0)
World	97.4	96.8	96.9	95.6	94.3	74.5*

Notes:
* Growth rates published as "provisional estimates" (based on coverage of *c*. 75 %).
** Growth rates published as "tentative estimates" (based on coverage of *c*. 40–*c*. 74%).
() Growth rates published but likely to change (based on coverage of less than 40%).
See text for estimation of coverage. A country is counted as covered only when a real observation is available, either from the preferred series or from a secondary series.

To address this kind of item non-response (i.e. gaps in the data for countries covered) we used a "model-based framework" to predict missing values.[40] This is necessary in order to hold the set of responding countries constant over time and so avoid the undesired effects associated with an unstable sample. Depending on the nature of the missing data points, we used several complementary approaches that are described in detail in Technical Appendix I of the 2010/11 edition of the *Global Wage Report*.

Treatment of total non-response

Response weights

To adjust for total non-response (when no time-series wage data are available for a given country) a "design-based framework" was used in which non-response was considered as a sampling problem. Because non-responding countries may have wage characteristics that differ from those of responding countries, non-response may introduce a bias into the final estimates. A standard approach to reduce the adverse effect of non-response is to calculate the propensity of response of different countries and then weight the data from responding countries by the inverse of their response propensity.[41] This implies that no imputations are made for non-responding countries.

In this framework, each country responds with a probability φ_j and it is assumed that countries respond independently of each other (Poisson sampling design). With the probabilities of response, φ_j, it is then possible to estimate the total, Y, of any variable y_j:

$$Y = \sum_{j \in U} y_j \tag{1}$$

by the estimator:

$$\hat{Y} = \sum_{j \in R} \frac{y_j}{\varphi_j} \tag{2}$$

where U is the population and R is the set of respondents. This estimator is unbiased if the assumptions are true (see Tillé, 2001). In our case, U is the universe of all countries and territories listed in table A1 and R are those "responding" countries for which we could find time-series wage data.

The difficulty is, however, that the response propensity of country j, φ_j, is generally not known and must itself be estimated. Many methods of estimation of the response propensity are available from the literature (see e.g. Tillé, 2001). In our case, the response propensity was estimated by relating the response or non-response of a given country to its number of employees and its labour productivity (or GDP per person employed in 2005 PPP$). This is based on the observation that wage statistics are more readily available for richer and larger countries than for poorer and smaller countries. We choose the number of employees and labour productivity since these variables are also used for calibration and size weighting (see below).[42]

For this purpose, we estimated a logistic regression with fixed effects as follows:

$$prob(response) = \Lambda(\alpha_h + \beta_1 x_{j2010} + \beta_2 n_{j2010}) \tag{3}$$

where x_{j2010} is ln(GDP per person employed in 2005 PPP$) of country j in the year 2010, n_{j2010} is ln(number of employees) in 2010, and Λ denotes the logistic cumulative distribution function (CDF).[43] The fixed effects, α_h, are dummies for each of the regions with incomplete data (Asia and the Pacific, Latin America and the Caribbean, Middle East, Africa), while the two remaining regions with complete data form the omitted benchmark category. The logistic regression had a universe of $N = 177$ cases and produced a pseudo $R^2 = 0.380$. The estimated parameters were then used to calculate the propensity of response of country j, φ_j.

The response weight for country j, ϕ_j, is then given by the inverse of a country's response propensity:

$$\phi_j = \frac{1}{\varphi_j} \tag{4}$$

Calibration factors

The final adjustment process, generally called calibration (see Särndal and Deville, 1992), is designed to ensure consistency of the estimate with known aggregates. This procedure ensures appropriate representation of the different regions in the final global estimate. In the present context, a single variable "number of employees", n, in a given year t was considered for calibration. In this simple case, the calibration factors, are given by γ_{jt}:

$$\gamma_{jt} = \frac{n_{ht}}{\hat{n}_{ht}}, j \in h \tag{5}$$

where h represents the region to which country j belongs, n_{ht} is the known number of employees in that region in year t, and $\hat{n}_{ht}$ is an estimate of total number of employees in the region and the same year that was obtained as a sum product of the uncalibrated weights and the employment data from the responding countries within each region.[44] The resulting calibration factors for the year 2010 were 1.00 (Developed economies; Eastern Europe and Central Asia), 0.975 (Asia and the Pacific), 1.045 (Latin America and the Caribbean), 1.042 (Africa) and 1.086 (Middle East). Since all calibration factors are either equal to or very close to 1, these results show that estimates $\hat{n}_{ht}$ were already very close to the known number of employees, n_{ht}, in each region. Note that the calibration process was repeated for each year so that the weight of each region in the global estimate changes over time in proportion to its approximate share in the global wage bill.

Calibrated response weights

The calibrated response weights, ϕ'_{jt}, are then obtained by multiplying the initial response weight with the calibration factor:

$$\phi'_{jt} = \phi_j \times \gamma_{jt} \tag{6}$$

The regional estimate of the number of employees based on the calibrated response weights is equal to the known total number of employees in that region in a given year. Thus, the calibrated response weights adjust for differences in non-response between regions. The calibrated response weights are equal to 1 in the regions where wage data were available for all countries (Developed economies; Eastern Europe and Central Asia). They are larger than 1 for small countries and countries with lower labour productivity since these are underrepresented among responding countries.

Estimating global and regional trends

One intuitive way to think of a global (or regional) wage trend is in terms of the evolution of the world's (or a region's) average wage. This would be in line with the concept used for other well-known estimates, such as regional GDP per capita growth (published by the World Bank) or the change in labour productivity (or GDP per person employed).

The global average wage, $\bar{y}$, at the point in time t can be obtained by dividing the sum of the national wage bills by the global number of employees:

$$\bar{y}_t = \frac{\sum_j n_{jt} \times \bar{y}_{jt}}{\sum_j n_{jt}} \tag{7}$$

where n_{jt} is the number of employees in country j and $\bar{y}_{jt}$ is the corresponding average wage of employees in country j, both at time t.The same operation can be repeated for the subsequent time period $t+1$ to obtain $\bar{y}^*_{t+1}$, using the deflated wages $\bar{y}^*_{t+1}$ and the number of employees n_{t+1}, where * refers to real wages. It is then straightforward to calculate the growth rate of the global average wage, r.

However, while this is a conceptually appealing way to estimate the global wage trends, it involves some difficulties that we cannot at present overcome. In particular, aggregating national wages, as done in equation (7), requires them to be converted into a common currency, such as PPP$. This conversion would make the estimates sensitive to revisions in PPP conversion factors. It would also require that national wage statistics be harmonized to a single concept of wages in order to make the level strictly comparable.[45]

More importantly, the change in the global average wage would also be influenced by composition effects that occur when the share of employees shifts between countries. For instance, if the number of paid employees fell in a country with high wages but expanded (or stayed constant) in a country of similar size with low wages, this would result in a fall of the global average wage (while wage levels remained constant in all countries). This effect makes changes in the global average wage difficult to interpret, as one would have to differentiate which part was due to changes in national average wages and which part was due to composition effects.

We therefore gave preference to an alternative specification to calculate global wage trends that maintains the intuitive appeal of the concept presented above but avoids its practical challenges. To ease interpretation, we also want to exclude effects that are due to changes in the composition of the world's employee population. We therefore avoid the danger of producing a statistical artefact of falling global average wages that could be caused by a shift in employment to low-wage countries (even when wages within countries are actually growing).

When the number of employees in each country is held constant, the global wage growth rate r_t can be expressed as a weighted average of the wage growth rates in the individual countries:

$$r_t = \sum_j w_{jt} \times r_{jt} \tag{8}$$

where r_{jt} is wage growth in country j at point in time t and the country weight, w_{jt}, is the share of country j in the global wage bill, as given by:

$$w_{jt} = n_{jt} \times \bar{y}_{jt} / \sum_j n_{jt} \times \bar{y}_{jt} \tag{9}$$

While we have data for the number of employees, n_{jt}, in all countries and relevant points in time from the ILO's Global Employment Trends Model,[46] we cannot estimate equation (9) directly since our wage data are not in a common currency. However, we can again draw on standard economic theory, which suggests that average wages vary roughly in line with labour productivity across countries.[47] We can thus estimate $\bar{y}_{jt}$ as a fixed proportion of labour productivity, LP:

$$\hat{y}_{jt} = \alpha \times \mathrm{LP}_{jt} \tag{10}$$

where α is the average ratio of wages over labour productivity. We can therefore estimate the weight as:

$$\hat{w}_{jt} = n_{jt} \times \alpha \times \mathrm{LP}_{jt} \,/\, \sum_j n_{jt} \times \alpha \times \mathrm{LP}_{jt} \tag{11}$$

which is equal to:

$$\hat{w}_{jt} = n_{jt} \times \mathrm{LP}_{jt} \,/\, \sum_j n_{jt} \times \mathrm{LP}_{jt} \tag{12}$$

Substituting $\hat{w}_{jt}$ for w_{jt} and introducing the calibrated response weight, ϕ'_j, into equation (8) gives us the final equation used to estimate global wage growth:

$$r_t = \frac{\sum_j \phi'_j \times \hat{w}_{jt} \times r_{jt}}{\sum_j \phi'_j \times \hat{w}_{jt}} \tag{13}$$

and for regional wage growth:

$$r_{ht} = \frac{\sum_j \phi'_j \times \hat{w}_{jt} \times r_{jt}}{\sum_j \phi'_j \times \hat{w}_{jt}}, j \in h \tag{13'}$$

where h is the region of which country j is part. As can be seen from equations (13) and (13′), global and regional wage growth rates are the weighted averages of the national wage trends, where ϕ'_j corrects for differences in response propensities between countries.

Appendix II

How a divergence between labour productivity and wages influences unit labour costs and the labour income share

The widening gap between productivity gains and increases in real wages in many developed economies was highlighted by the *Global Wage Report 2010/11*. *Labour productivity* sets the output of a production process in relation to the input used to generate it – in this case, the labour input. It is commonly measured as either value added per employed person or per hour worked. The hour-based measure has the advantage that it is not influenced by changes in output that are due to variations in working hours. However, reliable information on hours worked is not always available, so value added per employed person is often the preferred measure (as, for example, is the case with the Millennium Development Goals Indicator "labour productivity"; see Luebker, 2011). Organizations such as the OECD therefore publish both indicators (see McKenzie and Brackfield, 2008). Labour productivity is always measured in real terms; hence the measure for value added needs to be expressed in constant currency prices (i.e. adjusted for inflation, using the double-deflation method where both inputs and outputs are valued in constant prices). However, since the implicit GDP deflator might diverge from the consumer prices index (which is used to deflate wages) it can sometimes be useful to compare nominal value added and nominal wages.

The two concepts "wages" and "compensation of employees" are closely related. The term "wages", as used in the *Global Wage Report*, refers to total gross remuneration, including regular bonuses, received by employees during a specified period of time for both time worked and time not worked, such as paid annual leave and paid sick leave. Essentially, it corresponds to the concept of "total cash remuneration", which is the major component of income related to paid employment. It excludes employers' social security contributions. This is the major difference from "compensation of employees" as found in the UN System of National Accounts (2008). This is made up of two components, namely "wages and salaries" (which corresponds to the concept of wages in the *Global Wage Report*) and "employers' social contributions" to pension and other social security schemes. The labour income share (LS) relates compensation of employees (CoE) to total value added (GDP). The unadjusted measure is obtained by dividing total compensation by total value added, either at national or at sectoral level:

$$LS = \frac{CoE}{GDP} \tag{1}$$

Alternatively, one can calculate the labour income share as compensation per worker over value added per worker:

$$LS = \frac{CoE / worker}{GDP / worker} \quad (1')$$

Readers will recognize that the denominator – GDP per worker – corresponds to labour productivity as defined above. However, the numerator does not entirely match the concept of average wages as it is used in the *Global Wage Report*. First, CoE (unlike wages) also includes employers' social contributions. Secondly, "average wages" refers only to employees (and not to all workers, a term that also includes self-employed persons). Equation (1′) above can be rewritten so that it relates average wages directly to labour productivity:

$$LS = \frac{\alpha}{\beta} \times \frac{wage / employee}{LP} \quad (1'')$$

where α stands for CoE / wages and β for workers / employees. A common procedure (used also in Part II of the *Global Wage Report*) is to adjust the labour share for the share of employees in total employment. The adjusted labour share (LS′) can then be written as:

$$LS' = \alpha \times \frac{wage / employee}{LP} \quad (1''')$$

Fortunately for analysts, the coefficient α is remarkably stable over time. This holds even for a country like Germany, which over the past 35 years has gone though substantial structural change, a reunification, and reforms designed to reduce employers' social contributions. Nonetheless, the coefficient of CoE over wages and salaries remained in a narrow range between 1.21 and 1.24 from 1976 to 2011 (see Federal Statistical Office, 2012, table 1.8). This means that changes in the labour share can be attributed almost entirely to changes in the relationship between average wages and labour productivity. The labour share is therefore a convenient statistic to track the disconnection between these two variables that has occurred in many countries over the past decade.

The labour share is closely linked to unit labour costs (ULC). These are commonly defined as the average cost of labour per unit of output. Although they are frequently used as an indicator for the competitiveness of an economy, the OECD cautions that "ULCs should not be interpreted as a comprehensive measure of competitiveness, but as a reflection of cost competitiveness".[48]

Unit labour costs are usually expressed in nominal terms by relating nominal labour costs to real value added:

$$nULC = \frac{nCoE}{rGDP} \quad (2)$$

where n and r denote nominal and real values, respectively. Real GDP is obtained by deflating nominal GDP by a price index P. An alternative way to calculate nominal unit labour costs is therefore to use the price index P alongside the nominal values for CoE and GDP:

$$nULC = \frac{nCoE}{nGDP} * P \tag{2'}$$

As can be seen from these two equations, nominal ULC can increase because nominal compensation of employees grows faster than nominal GDP, or because prices increase. Countries with high inflation will therefore usually see a faster increase in nominal unit labour costs than those with low inflation. This makes it difficult to compare nominal unit labour costs across countries that use different currencies.

The alternative is to calculate real unit labour costs, which sets the real (i.e. inflation-adjusted) cost of labour in relation to real output. In other words, both CoE and GDP need to be deflated with a price index *P*:

$$rULC = \frac{nCoE * {}^{1}/_{P}}{nGDP * {}^{1}/_{P}} = \frac{nCoE}{nGDP} \tag{3}$$

Since the price indices cancel each other out, real unit labour costs are therefore usually calculated on the basis of nominal values (OECD, 2008). This also avoids the spurious results that that can arise when the consumer price index (CPI) is used to deflate labour cost, but the producer price index (PPI) for GDP (see Fleck, Glaser and Sprague, 2011). For presentational purposes, unit labour costs are often expressed as an index that takes the value of 100 in a base year (e.g. 2005).

As it turns out, equation 3 for real unit labour costs is exactly the same as equation (1) for the labour income share. This is no coincidence, and in fact the terms "labour income share" and "real unit labour costs" are often used as synonyms (see McKenzie and Brackfield, 2008). What this implies is that policies to reduce real unit labour costs will in effect delink wages from productivity and reduce the labour income share (thereby increasing the capital income share).

Nominal unit labour costs can of course also fall as a result of a decline in the price index *P*. However, few policy-makers will aim for outright deflation – a phenomenon that made the Great Depression of the 1930s much worse and increases the real value of existing debts. When prices continue to rise, reducing nominal unit labour costs will therefore require an even sharper decline in the wage share than merely reducing real unit labour costs.

While a reduction in labour costs appears popular among some economic commentators, it is much less clear whether the implications for the functional income distribution have been thought though – and it remains unclear why increasing profits at the expense of wages should be good economic policy (the question addressed in Part II of the *Global Wage Report*).

Appendix III

Determinants of labour shares

Box A1 Data selection and estimation procedure: An econometric methodology

The methodology employed in the estimation procedure to determine the effects of different variables on labour shares is based on a causal framework that requires four basic steps. The dependent variable (labour income share) and independent variables (internal and external factors) are constructed by combining datasets (Step 1), carefully considering problems of misreporting and endogeneity (Step 2). The determinants of labour income shares are grouped according to the factors in figure 37 (Step 3) and the combination of the determinants (Step 4) underlines the specifications, leading to the estimates in tables A4 and A5.

Step 1: The following information sources were combined to construct the dependent variable and set of independent variables:

- **Dependent variable**: ILO/ILLS database for the construction of the main indicator on wage shares as proxy for labour income shares.
- **Deterministic factors**: AMECO database, OECD database, Chinese National Accounts, UNIDO Industrial Index, World Bank World Development Indicators (WB-WDI), PENN World Tables, EU-KLEMS database.
- **Complementary data** were also drawn direction from the studies of Aleksynska and Schindler (2011), Bassanini and Duval (2006) and Lane and Milesi-Ferretti (2007).

Treatment and nature of the data: The dependent variable and the determinants are estimated on an annual basis for the period 1970–2007 for 71 economies.

Step 2: The dependent variable is *total wage share,* which equals *total wage bill* divided by national income. It is constructed allowing for two adjustments:

- **Adjustment 1 (control for mis-reporting): Income data from the self-employed includes salaries and profits. To avoid overestimating the contribution from the self-employed (by excluding profits), the total wage bill is estimated as the sum of wages from "salaried employees" augmented by an element corresponding to the share of the self-employed in the workforce.Thus, employees act as counterfactuals to what would have been the salaries of the self-employed had they been wage workers (Gollin, 2002).**
- **Adjustment 2 (controlling endogeneity): The total wage bill includes the wages from the public sector closely related to the measure of government consumption (GC). The variable GC is included in the right-hand side of the causal relation to pick up the effect on changes in "total wage share". Thus, the adjusted measure of total wage share has to be further adjusted by subtracting GC from the total wage bill: the second adjustment makes GC (in the right-hand side) exogenous to total wage share (in the left-hand side).**

Box A1 Data selection and estimation procedure (continued)

Apply adjustment 1 and adjustment 2: The final dependent variable is the private sector total wage bill, adjusted for the self-employed, as percentage of national income.

Step 3:The estimating procedure considers five sets of independent factors as key determinants of labour income share:

- **Real GDP growth is included to control for cyclic and structural changes and might affect the secular trend of the share of functional income. Real GDP growth captures within country heterogeneity that varies derministically over time.**
- **Technological progress: industrial share of GDP, agro-fishery share of GDP, average labour productivity and – for developed economies – capital–labour share and ICT–capital shares. In terms of capital–labour share, the measure is used exclusively for advanced economies where the use of average labour productivity does not help capture technological progress due to the homogeneity of average labour productivity between economies and over time. Thus, in the estimates capital–labour share (for advanced economies only) is measured as the value of the total capital services as a ratio of the total number of employees in that sector: it is therefore a measure of average labour productivity with exclusive reference to capital.**
- **Financialization (global financialization): constructed as total external assets plus external liabilities of an economy as share of GDP. This is the standard method followed in the literature to measure the importance of the financial sector for an economy (see European Commission,2007; Rodrick, 1997; Stockhammer, forthcoming).**
- **Globalization: trade openness (total exports and imports as share of GDP) and terms of trade (unit value of exports to unit value of imports).**
- **Government consumption as share of GDP (as proxy for the welfare state).**
- **Labour market institutions: union density, a minimum wage index, unemployment benefits indicators (replacement rates and coverage), advance notice period for unemployment, severance payments and controls for supply-side effects (labour force and population).**

Step 4: The model assumes a static causal relationship between the variables. Estimates are constructed by pooling the data available from an unbalanced panel (71 countries, with at most 37 years of observations from each country) while controlling for individual fixed effects. Accordingly, the model can be expressed as follows:

$$WSAP_{it} = F[FIN_{it}, GLOB_{it}, TECH_{it}, WFST_{it}, LMI_{it}; e_{it}]$$

i; country among n countries
t; time period of observation
e; stochastic shocks

Including or excluding particular sets of variables allows for two distinct sets of specifications:

- **Baseline specification:** ignores labour market institutional variables (LMI) to enable a better understanding of the joint effects of globalization and the bargaining power of employees (table A4)
- **Augmented baseline specification:** allows each of the five variables identified as labour market indicators in Step 3 to enter the baseline specification, leading to new set of estimates (table A5).

Results and interpretation

Table A4 shows estimates for the baseline specification for three groups of countries: all economies (71 economies), industrialized economies (28 OECD economies) and developing economies (9 economies). This distinction is important from both conceptual and practical points of view. High-income OECD economies have more homogeneous labour markets and industrial structures, and have better-quality data over a longer time-span. These conditions allow us to work on an extended model with all of the potential factors without much risk of statistical errors or unreliability (e.g. statistical "noise"). Thus, a full model specification is used for industrialized economies. The impact of globalization is captured by the variables "trade openness" and "terms of trade", where the former measures the exposure to the global market and the latter measures the relative competitiveness of a country in international trade. The impact of "financial globalization" is captured by the sum of external assets and external liabilities in GDP (from Lane and Milesi-Ferretti, 2007). Both government consumption and union density are also included.

However, such an approach is not feasible for developing economies, largely because of the limitations on available data, particularly relating to union density. A different model specification is thus used, including some new variables – share of the industrial sector, share of the agro-forestry and labour productivity – to control for the effects of technological progress and structural change. When all 71 countries are taken together in the regression, the country variations between developed and developing economies are such that industry share, agro-forestry share and labour productivity are considered sufficient to capture the impacts of technology and structural change on the labour income share. However, in the case of developed economies these three variables are too homogeneous and do not identify the heterogeneity in technological gaps between countries in this group. Instead, the variables capital–labour ratio and capital–service ratio are used to capture such gaps when estimating the baseline specification for the 28 OECD high-income countries. Finally, real economic growth is included to control for the short-run business cycle adjustment on wage setting behaviour; the negative sign is consistent with the finding that wages are countercyclical.

All estimates shown in table A4 can be read in terms of the magnitude of the impact (the value of the coefficients) and the direction of the impact (the sign). The estimates confirm the role of technology and globalization in international trade and financial markets in reducing the labour income share in both developed and developing economies. Interestingly, the impact is similar in magnitude irrespective of country grouping. Positive changes in government consumption increase the labour income share in both developed and developing economies. However, the impact is smaller in magnitude when the estimates cover all 71 economies, potentially pointing to the relative variability of government consumption between developed and developing countries as determinant of labour income shares.[49] Likewise, the coefficient for union density (for OECD economies) indicates the positive effect of bargaining power on labour income shares.[50]

Using the estimates based on the 71 countries together, we see that both increasing levels of industrialization and increases in the capital–labour ratio (both measures of capital augmentation through technological progress) have an adverse effect on labour income shares, as expected and consistently with the findings of previous studies on the topic

(IMF, 2007; Kumhof and Rainciere, 2011; IMF 2010; OECD, 2012b).[51] Nevertheless, in the case of developing economies the coefficients for industrialization and labour productivity imply a positive relationship between technological progress and labour income shares. This could be an indicator of the catching-up effect that some of these economies have experienced – at least up to 2007 – as explained in the IMF report on the globalization of labour (IMF, 2007). During the period of catching up, when economies are shifting their emphasis from agricultural to industrial sectors, the resulting tightening of the labour market may push wages up, as labour productivity increases and technology is upgraded. Similar findings have recently been confirmed by other studies (e.g. OECD, 2012b).

The baseline specification can be further augmented to include indicators for labour market institutions (LMIs), i.e. those variables that (in addition to union density) are directly indicative of the strength of the bargaining process in determining the share of income that goes to labour. Table A5 shows the result of running various specifications where each LMI has been added as an additional factor to the baseline specification explained and tabulated in table A4. The reason for adding *each* of the LMI indicators *separately* is twofold. First, given the positive impact of unionization density on labour wage shares, adding independent indicators that are likely to be the cause of unionization allows better understanding of the possible transition mechanisms between unionization (bargaining power) and the labour share of income. Secondly, the LMIs are likely to be highly correlated, so that adding each separately avoids multicollinearity problems in identification of the estimated parameters.

The estimates are based on all 71 economies in the sample. In practice the estimates show that no single variable on its own is causal to change in the labour income share: that is, the variability within each variable between countries means that we cannot detect significance for any one of the LMIs. It must be pointed out that even when the substantive legal provisions remain unchanged (e.g. the level of minimum wages and unemployment benefits), it is still possible for their effectiveness to be reduced as more workers are excluded from their coverage. De facto deregulation has taken place in many countries with a growing number of non-standard workers and the further segmentation of the labour market; this might explain the finding of no significance for LMI variables in table A5. It is important to point out that the LMI variables employed in the present analysis are not new and have been widely used in empirical studies (IMF, 2007; European Commission, 2007; OECD, 2012b);[52] as in this report, the estimates in similar studies are not statistically significant.

In table A4 unionization density had a positive impact on the labour share of income; the lack of unionization in developing economies implies that we cannot identify this variable in the specifications proposed in table A5. In order to understand whether the results in table A5 are the result of poor data quality in developing economies, an alternative specification was run based only on the 28 OECD high-income economies, using all seven LMI variables *simultaneously* and adding the variable "union density". The resulting coefficient did not change the argument: the five variables that control for strength of LMIs were not significant and only "union density" had a positive and significant effect on the determination of the labour share of income. Therefore, it is clear that it is unionization – and not the outcomes that result from unionization – that provides a cushion for falling labour income shares in the presence of globalization and financialization.

Finally, other specifications were tried adding variables that control for possible structural changes such as unemployment rate, the volatility of exchange rates and financial reforms.[53] Increases in unemployment were found to have strong negative impacts on the labour share, which should not come as a surprise given the downward pressure on wages and the weakening of workers' bargaining position in the presence of higher rates of unemployment. Likewise, an increase in the riskiness of international trade (as expressed by volatility in exchange rate) may reduce the labour share: this finding is consistent with some earlier studies (e.g. Jayadev, 2007; IILS, 2011). Finally, financial liberalization has the effect of tilting the functional income distribution from labour to capital. When the credit control index developed by Abiad et al. – which measures liberalization in credit control – is included in the model, the effect is to reduce the labour share (Abiad, Detragiache and Tressel, 2008), a finding that is consistent with the predictions of Obstfeld and Rogoff (Obstfeld and Rogoff, 2009). Similar impacts (albeit of varying significance) are found when the baseline specification includes other indices of financial reform such as credit controls, interest rate controls, entry barriers, privatization, international capital flows and security markets.

Table A4 The factors influencing the adjusted labour income shares

	Dependent variable: Adjusted labour income shares		
Factors	All economies (28 OECD, 3 non-OECD high-income, 27 emerging, 13 developing)	Industrialized economies (28 OECD)	Developing economies (9)
Real GDP growth	-11.2** (2.97)	-16.4** (3.2)	-26.6** (13.0)
Financial globalization (1)	-3.1** (0.59)	-2.4** (0.7)	-5.0 (3.6)
Trade openness	-6.2** (1.40)	-5.9** (1.8)	-5.9** (6.8)
Terms of trade	-4.2** (1.30)	-4.5** (1.8)	••
Government consumption (% of GDP)	0.4** (0.19)	0.9** (0.2)	0.8** (0.4)
Industrial sector (% of GDP)	-0.3** (0.07)	••	0.6** (0.2)
Agro-forestry sector (% of GDP)	-0.1 (0.10)	••	-0.07 (0.2)
Average labour productivity (1)	-2.4 (2.08)	••	23.7** (9.4)
Union density		0.1* (0.06)	
Capital–labour ratio (1)		-7.0* (3.7)	
Capital services (% of GDP) (1)		1.4 (0.9)	
Diagnostics			
Number of observations	1,450	470	101
Adjusted R-square	0.98	0.94	0.99
Durbin–Watson D-statistic	1.72	1.81	2.04

Note: All models employ a fixed effect estimation procedure on the pool panel data. Financial globalization measures external assets plus external liabilities divided by GDP; trade openness measures exports plus imports divided by GDP; terms of trade measures export unit value relative to import unit value; average labour productivity measures PPP-converted GDP per worker at constant prices; government consumption is expressed as % of GDP; industrial sector measures all industrial sectors' added values as percentage of GDP; agro-forestry sector as % of GDP includes the value added by forestry, hunting, fishing, crop cultivation and livestock production; union density measures the proportion of the working population unionized; capital–labour ratio measures total capital services divided by the number of workers; capital services measures information communication and technology investment divided by gross value added.

(1) These variables enter in logarithmic form. ** Indicates significance at the 5% level; * indicates significance at 10% level. Bracketed numbers are standard errors.

Source: ILO estimates (Stockhammer, forthcoming).

Table A5 The impact of external factors on adjusted labour income shares

Baseline specification augmented by each of the following labour market indicators (LMI)	Dependent variable: Adjusted labour income shares				
	All economies (28 OECD, 3 non-OECD high-income, 27 emerging, 13 developing)	No. of observations	No. of variables	Adjusted R-square	Durbin–Watson D-statistic
Minimum wage index	-0.5 (1.7)	718	8	0.97	1.7
Unemployment benefits, replacement rates	-2.5 (1.9)	1,007	8	0.98	1.7
Unemployment benefits, coverage	0.5 (0.8)	878	8	0.98	1.7
Advance notice period after 4 years of service	-1.2 (0.8)	1,026	8	0.98	1.7
Severance pay after 4 years of service	0.1 (0.4)	1,026	8	0.98	1.7
Size of the labour force [(1)]	5.0 (3.7)	1,242	8	0.98	1.7
Size of the population [(1)]	-9.7 (6.5)	1,450	8	0.98	1.7

Note: All models employ a fixed effect estimation procedure on the pool unbalanced panel data with information from 1970 to 2007. The minimum wage index measures the ratio between the minimum wage and the mean wage (Kaitz Index).

[(1)] These variables enter in logarithmic form. ** Indicates significance at the 5% level; * indicates significance at 10% level. Bracketed numbers are standard errors.

Source: ILO estimates (Stockhammer, forthcoming).

Table A6 Description of countries included in the estimation of tables A4 and A5 and box A1

Groups	Individual countries
High-income OECD members (28 countries)	**Criteria: US$12,276 or more income per capita and OECD members** Australia, Austria, Belgium, Canada, Czech Republic, Denmark, Estonia, Finland, France, Germany, Greece, Hungary, Iceland, Ireland, Italy, Japan, Luxembourg, Netherlands, New Zealand, Norway, Poland, Portugal, Slovakia, Spain, Sweden, Switzerland, United Kingdom, United States
Non-OECD high-income (31 countries)	**Criteria: US$12,276 or more income per capita** High-income OECD members listed above (28) and Hong Kong, Kuwait and Oman
Upper–middle-income (27 countries)	**Criteria: US$3,976–12,275 income per capita** Algeria, Argentina, Azerbaijan, Belarus, Botswana, Brazil, Bulgaria, Chile, China, Colombia, Costa Rica, Iran, Jordan, Latvia, Lithuania, Mauritius, Mexico, Namibia, Panama, Peru, Russia, South Africa, South Korea, Thailand, Tunisia, Turkey, Venezuela
Lower–middle-income (9 countries)	**Criteria: US$1,006–3,975 income per capita** Armenia, Côte d'Ivoire, Egypt, India, Moldova, Mongolia, Nigeria, Philippines, Sri Lanka
Low-income (4 countries)	**Criteria: US$1,005 or below income per capita** Kenya, Kyrgyzstan, Niger, Tanzania

Source: ILO estimates (Stockhammer, forthcoming).

Explaining the decomposition of labour income shares in figure 38

1. Assume a particular specification that links a set of covariates to the wage share (WS) observed for 71 economies (i) for the years 1970 to 2007. These variables are GDP growth, *R*, technology, *TH*, globalization, *G*, financialization, *F*, government consumption, *GC*, and unionization, *U*:

$$ws_{it} = \beta_1 R_{it} + \beta_2 G_{it} + \beta 3F_{it} + \beta_4 TH_{it} + \beta_5 GC_{it} + \beta_6 U_{it} + residual_{it} + f_i$$
$$\text{where} \quad (1)$$
$$i;\ country,\ t = time,\ f_i : fixed\ effects$$

2. Run the model to get the coefficients in expression (1). This is done allowing for all observations to enter as if we had a cross section. Once the model is estimated we can interpret expression (1) as follows in expression (2):

Following table A1:
Developed:

$$ws_{it} = -16.4 \times R_{it} - \underbrace{(5.9 \times OPEN_{it} + 4.5 \times TOT)}_{G_{it}} - 2.4 \times F_{it} - 7.0 \times TH_{it} + 0.9 \times GC_{it} + 0.1 \times U_{it} + \hat{e}_{it}$$
$$\text{where}$$
$$OPEN:\ trade\ openness,\ TOT:\ terms\ of\ trade \quad (2)$$

Developing:

$$ws_{it} = -26.6 \times R_{it} - 5.9 \times TOT - 5.0 \times F_{it} + \underbrace{(0.6 \times IND_{it} + 23.7 \times LP_{it} - 0.7 \times AG_{it})}_{TH_{ij}} + 0.8 \times GC_{it} + e_{it}$$
$$\text{where}$$
$$IND:\ industrial\ sector,\ LP:\ labour\ productivity,$$
$$AG:\ agricultural\ production$$

3. The decomposition as shown in figure 38 is based on specifications and coefficients in expression (2). Let's take 'developed economies' as example:
   1. Select two periods over time: 1990–94 and 2000–04.
   2. For each period estimate the average of each variable (G, F, TH, C and U) as if the average between countries emulates some 'hypothetical' country. The variable 'real GPD growth' has not changed over the two selected periods so that its contribution to the final decomposition is neglible (can be ignored).
   3. Each of the averages is weighted by the corresponding (estimated) coefficient as given in expression (2). For example, F is measured as the logarithm of the sum of external assets and external liabilities: let's say the average of F for all economies and for the period 1990–94 gives a total of 0.04 whereas for the period 2000–04 the average is 1.5. Then, each of these numbers is weighted by the same coefficient value of -2.4.

4. Taking differences between the two weighted values – i.e., (1.5)(-2.4)-(0.06)(-2.4) = -3.3 – shows the contribution of the variable 'financialization' (or global financialization) in figure 38.
5. Doing the same for each of the variables and adding the total provides the "predicted" difference between periods for the wage share. This equals (approximately) -7.1, i.e., between the periods 1990–94 and 2000–04 the wage share has decreased by 7.1 per cent. The same applies to developing economies in the second set of bars for figure 38: in this case the average change in WS for the 'hypothetical' economy in the developing world is -2 per cent.

Appendix IV

The effect of labour share on aggregate demand

Box A2 Data, estimation and simulations

Our simulations on the effects of lower labour shares on components of aggregate demand are based on elasticity estimates that assume single equations to explain (independently) each of the items that integrate aggregate demand, namely **GC** (government consumption), **C** (aggregate domestic private consumption on goods and services), **I** (aggregate private investment) and **NX** (aggregate net exports, i.e. the value of exports minus imports). It is assumed that functional income shares affect each of the components in the identity that explains national income **Y** (i.e. **Y = GC + C + I + NX**) but feedback effects between the components are not accounted for when providing final simulation effects. The simplification reduces the problem of using untestable assumptions on a system of equations; avoiding such assumptions allows for a clear policy-oriented interpretation of the results. The estimation process consists of three steps:

Step 1: Selecting the countries, the time-span and the databases

- **16 economies:** Eurozone (12 core high-income economies), Argentina, Australia, Canada, China, France, Germany, India, Italy, Japan, Mexico, Republic of Korea, South Africa, Turkey, United Kingdom, United States.
- **Time series periods:** 1960–2007 for developed economies; 1970–2007 for developing economies; 1978–2007 for China. The period of the crisis is omitted.
- **Dependent variables: Growth in** private consumption, investment, net exports.
- **Independent (causal) variables:** indicators of labour income shares and profit income shares. The labour income share (or labour wage share, LWS) has been adjusted in the same form as described in step 2 of Appendix III. Capital (or profit) income shares follow by construction from LWS: CIS = 1 – LWS. Other indicators include industrial share (IND), agricultural share (AGR), terms of trade (TOT), World GDP (wGDP), import prices (MP), export prices (XP), domestic prices (P), unit labour cost (ULC).
- **Databases and sources**: ILO/IILS, World Bank WDI, UNIDO; for Argentina and South Africa, Lindenboim et al. (2011) and UN National Accounts; for China, Zhou et al. (2010).

Step 2: Specification of long-run relationship between labour income shares and capital income shares and the dependent variables (C, I, NX):

The following specifications are applied to each economy independently:

CONSUMPTION: $C_t = F[LWS_t, CIS_t, IND_t, AGR_t; e_t]$

INVESTMENT: $I_t = F[CIS_t, IND_t, AGR_t; e_t]$

EXPORTS: $M_t = F[TOT_t, wGDP_t, MP_t, P_t, ULC_t; e_t]$

IMPORTS: $X_t = F[TOT_t, wGDP_t, XP_t, P_t, ULC_t; e_t]$

Box A2 Data, estimation and simulations (continued)

Assumptions:

- Single equation approach
- Long run relationship where the LWS and the CIS are exogenous to the aggregate demand component.

Step 3: Simulations

Effect of a 1 per cent decrease on LWS (1 per cent increase in CIS) on C, I, NX:

Estimate each of the causal relations in step 2, using log transformation in all variables, to find the elasticities (coefficients) of each variable included in the specification.

Apply the elasticities to the identities that explain each of the aggregated demand items (C, I, NX) in the form of marginal changes with respect to national income. Take the mean average change of consumption, income and net exports to be the mean average change observed over the period (in real terms).

Simultaneous decrease of 1 per cent LWS (1 per cent increase in CIS) on each country's total aggregate private demand:

Assume *n* economies where economy *i* is a trade partner of all other *j* economies in *n*. The simultaneous effect on a country's aggregated demand (AD) of a change in LWS in all *n* economies for an economy *i* is given as the sum of the following 4 components:

$$\%\Delta AD_i = \begin{Bmatrix} \%\Delta GDP_i \\ + \\ \%\Delta AD_i \text{ given a } \%\Delta LWS_i \\ + \\ \text{National Multiplier effect on } AD_i \\ + \\ \sum_j \left(\%\Delta NX_j \text{ given a } \%\Delta LWS_j\right) \end{Bmatrix}$$

Results and interpretation

Our estimation strategy consists in using a dynamic framework on time series data for the period 1960–2007 to estimate elasticities of labour income shares for 16 economic units, individually, for each economy and for each of the three items in aggregate demand. The elasticities measure how responsive each of the aggregate demand components is to changes in labour income share. The demand side interpretation of national income assumes the existence of stable, long-run equilibrium between aggregate demand and labour income share. On the other hand, the modelling strategy assumes no feedback effects between the different aggregate demand components (consumption, investment and net exports) and a change in labour income shares. The simplification comes at the cost of potential imprecisions in the estimate of the elasticities. On the other hand, estimating single equations for each economy has the advantage that it avoids having to make untestable identifying assumptions that further complicate the interpretation of the results for the purpose of policy advice.[54] It is important to point out the duality in the estimation procedure: an elasticity that measures the impact of a change on any given item (say, investment) for a 1 per cent fall (increase) in labour income share is equivalent to measuring the change on the same item for a 1 per cent increase (fall) in capital (i.e. profit) income share. Government consumption has been ignored because by definition government consumption is the same as public employment income share. In this respect, the wage shares in the empirical estimates that follow have been adjusted as described above.

The estimated elasticities are used in the empirical analysis in two different forms. First, they are used to simulate the change in consumption, investment and net exports (relative to GDP) caused by a 1 per cent fall in labour income share; this is simply done by multiplying the estimated elasticities by the observed mean value of the corresponding items in aggregate demand weighted by the factor prices. Second, the estimated elasticities are used in a more general framework to simulate the change in aggregate demand for any given economy (among the 16 economic units) if all other 15 economic units experienced a simultaneous 1 per cent fall in labour income share: the feedback effect is simulated assuming that each country's fall in labour income share has a measurable impact on its net exports.

Figure A1 shows the results of simulating the impact of a 1 per cent fall in labour income shares on each of the components of aggregate demand. Compared to investment and net exports, the response of private consumption of domestic goods is negative and substantial across all economic units: in this case it is not possible to distinguish between developed and developing economies as all seem to suffer losses of similar magnitude. With the exceptions of Argentina, Australia and South Africa, all countries and the eurozone as a whole would experience a drop in consumption of 0.3 per cent or more. In the case of economies with significantly large populations and, therefore, large internal markets (the eurozone, China, Germany, Mexico, Turkey, the United States), the drop in consumption is greater, ranging between 0.4 per cent and 0.5 per cent.

Whereas consumption falls, investment is positively affected by a decline in labour income share in all but six economic units, and in these the effect is non-zero but negligent: these are Argentina, China, India, the Republic of Korea, Turkey and the United States. One possible reason why investment is not sensitive to a fall in labour income share (i.e. to an increase in the profit income shares) in emerging economies is the lack of a correlation between firms' profits and overall investment, because in these countries public industrial policies and public investment are the drivers of infrastructure and industrial development. Thus, for most emerging economies, high investment rates are part of the authorities' attempt to create an optimal business environment – with a view to catching up in the global market – whereas short-term private profit shares have only weak effects on investment rates (Akyüz et al., 1998). The only advanced economy where an increase in profit share shows zero impact on investment is the United States: in an earlier study by Onaran et al. (2011), the inclusion of interest and dividend payments in the definition of investment for the United States was found to have confounding effects that made it impossible to detect the significance of an increase in capital income share (a drop in labour income share) for investment. The same might be happening in the present set of estimates.[55] For all other developed economies, the impact of a 1 per cent fall in labour income share (i.e. a 1 per cent increase in capital income share) is to increase investment by 0.1 per cent or more. The effect is greatest in the eurozone (0.3 per cent), Germany (0.38 per cent) and Japan (0.29 per cent).

In the case of net exports, figure A1(c) shows that a 1 per cent drop in labour income share induces an increase in net exports in all countries. It is important to note that in the case of net exports the magnitude is estimated with a composite of elasticities that depend on the relative prices of exports and imports, the degree of openness of the economy and price elasticity at home.[56] The effects are larger for developing countries such as Mexico and South Africa and, as expected, extraordinarily high in China as this is the most aggressive export-led economy in the global market. It is illustrative to point out that the estimate of a 2 per cent increase in net exports for China (given a 1 per cent drop in labour income share in China) is composed of 1.1 per cent increase in the share of exports (in GDP) and a 0.9 per cent decline in import share (of GDP). These marked effects are related to several factors that characterize the Chinese labour market. First, the elasticity of prices with respect to unit labour costs is the highest in the world, indicating a highly labour-intensive export structure with high mark-ups. Second, the elasticity of exports with respect to relative prices is again the highest in the world, reflecting the highly price-elastic character of the demand for Chinese exports, which rely heavily on consumer goods such as textiles. Finally, the elasticity of imports with respect to relative prices is the second highest in the world after South Africa. This last point might also explain why South Africa shows the second highest impact on net exports among the 16 economic units of a 1 per cent drop in labour income share (figure A1(c)).

One might be tempted to add up all the independent effects for each of the economic units to illustrate the overall impact of a 1 per cent drop in labour income shares on private aggregate demand. This would be misleading, for figure A1 and the estimates leading to it ignore the feedback effects that exist between consumption, investment and net exports. Nevertheless, the estimates presented in figure A1 are informative: for most of the economies considered, the impact of lowering the labour share of income – say, by reducing wages below average productivity to gain competitiveness – is likely to have such a negative effect on domestic consumption (domestically traded goods and services) that it would require a massive response in the form of domestic investment and net exports to offset the adverse impact on aggregate demand. The findings are in line with those of Felipe and Kumar, who find that cutting unit labour costs (reducing the labour income share) is detrimental to economies that do not have a niche for their basket of exports in the global market: there is no gain in cutting unit labour costs when they compete with China to place a similar basket of exports in the global economy, for that cut in unit labour costs will simply deepen a county's recession further through the adverse effect on consumption (reducing effective demand) and investment (widening the technological gap) (Felipe and Kumar, 2011).

Figure A1 Effect of a 1% decrease in labour income share on private consumption of domestic goods and services, investment and net exports: (a) private consumption of goods and services; (b) investment; (c) net exports

	Private consumption	Investment	Net exports
Euro area-12	↘ (-0.439)	↗ (0.299)	↗ (0.057)
Argentina	↘ (-0.153)	→ (0.015)	↗ (0.192)
Australia	↘ (-0.256)	↗ (0.174)	↗ (0.272)
Canada	↘ (-0.326)	↗ (0.182)	↗ (0.266)
China	↘ (-0.412)	→ (0.000)	↗↗ (1.986)
France	↘ (-0.305)	↗ (0.088)	↗ (0.198)
Germany	↘ (-0.501)	↗ (0.376)	↗ (0.096)
India	↘ (-0.291)	→ (0.000)	↗ (0.310)
Italy	↘ (-0.356)	↗ (0.130)	↗ (0.126)
Japan	↘ (-0.353)	↗ (0.284)	↗ (0.055)
Mexico	↘ (-0.438)	↗ (0.153)	↗ (0.381)
Republic of Korea	↘ (-0.422)	→ (0.000)	↗ (0.359)
South Africa	↘ (-0.145)	↗ (0.129)	↗ (0.506)
Turkey	↘ (-0.491)	→ (0.000)	↗ (0.283)
United Kingdon	↘ (-0.303)	↗ (0.120)	↗ (0.037)
United States	↘ (-0.426)	→ (0.000)	↗ (0.037)

Note: The bracketed value shows the % change in each of the corresponding items: % change in private consumption of goods and services, % change in investment goods, % consumption of exports value minus import value (net export).

Source: Onaran and Galanis, forthcoming.

Notes

Major trends in wages

1 For unemployment rates in individual countries, see ILO, 2011c.

2 "Paid employees" excludes own-account workers, contributing family workers, members of workers' cooperatives and workers unclassifiable by status. Wages are defined in Appendix I.

3 See ILO, 2012b. An alternative measure of wages would have been hourly wages, but these are available for only a limited number of countries with more advanced statistical systems.

4 Estimates including China may somewhat overstate global wage growth, given that the only wage series which covers the entire period from 2006 to 2012 refers only to "urban units", which in practice cover mostly State-owned enterprises, collective-owned units and other type of companies linked to the State. A new series published in the China Yearbook of Statistics now provides separate estimates of annual wages paid to employees in "urban private units", but this series only started in 2009 and no series is available that covers all employees.

5 Work-sharing programmes are also known as "short-time work" or as "partial" or "technical" unemployment (see Messenger, 2009).

6 Work-sharing programmes have been implemented in Argentina, Austria, Bulgaria, Canada, Chile, Croatia, the Czech Republic, Belgium, France, Germany, Hungary, Mexico, the Netherlands, Poland, Romania, Serbia (at company level only), Slovakia, Slovenia, South Africa, Switzerland, Turkey and Uruguay; small programmes have been implemented in a number of individual states in the United States (see ILO, 2011a). For further information regarding work-sharing measures in middle-income countries, see also Messenger and Rodríguez, 2010).

7 Preliminary estimates, using preliminary quarterly data from 30 selected developed economies for which data are available, suggest that real average wages are likely to grow by about 0 per cent in developed economies in 2012.

8 Figure 9 also confirms that higher inflation in 2008 was not caused by higher nominal wage demands, as nominal wages continued to grow at the same (or even a slightly slower) rate as in 2007. On the contrary: the higher prices were passed on to workers, who as a result received lower real wages. The figure also suggests that positive wage growth in 2009 prevented a fuller price deflation in 2009.

9 While there are a number of different ways to measure labour productivity, they all define economic output in relation to labour input (see OECD, 2001). In line with the United Nations' Millennium Development Goals, this report uses GDP per person employed as a simple measure of labour productivity. While more

refined approaches that adjust for hours worked are often useful for single-country studies (see e.g. the labour productivity figures published by the US Bureau of Labor Statistics at http://www.bls.gov/lpc/ [accessed 17 Sep. 2012]), our simple measure is more appropriate for studies such as the Global Wage Report that cover a large number of countries, for many of which no reliable data on hours worked are available.

10 For trends in Ukraine between 1992 and 2002 see Ganguli and Terrell, 2006; for more recent trends, see ILO, 2011d.

11 The proportion of people available to work full-time but working shorter hours shot up from 4.4 per cent in 2007 to 10.6 per cent in 2008 and to 19.4 per cent in 2009, before declining again to 12.3 per cent in the first half of 2010.

12 Argentina identified some inconsistencies in its wage series which could not be resolved before publication of this report; for this reason, the decision was made not to publish them in this edition of the report.

13 The members of the GCC are Bahrain, Qatar, Kuwait, Oman, Saudi Arabia and the United Arab Emirates.

14 The 2008 ILO Declaration on Social Justice for a Fair Globalization highlights as part of its Decent Work Agenda the promotion of "policies in regard to wages and earnings, hours and other conditions of work, designed to ensure a just share of the fruits of progress to all and a minimum living wage to all employed and in need of such protection" (ILO, 2008a, p. 10). The 2009 Global Jobs Pact also encouraged governments to "consider options such as minimum wages that can reduce poverty and inequity, increase demand and contribute to economic stability" (ILO, 2009, p. 7).

15 See the Minimum Wage Fixing Convention, 1970 (No. 131).

16 From €877 per month (i.e. €751 payable over 14 months) to €684 per month.

17 In early 2010, the ILO and the World Bank conducted a joint survey of policy responses to the crisis in 77 countries over a two-year period (mid-2008 to end 2010). The resulting database and the joint report can be seen at http://ww.ilo.org/crisis-inventory [accessed 17 Sep. 2012]. The minimum wage was one of 62 policy tools surveyed. Several explanations were put forward for the variation among countries, including the institutional setting of the minimum wage which makes it easy – and sometimes compulsory – to adjust its level (Bonnet, Saget and Weber, 2012).

18 The US$1.25 international poverty line corresponds to the mean national poverty line of 15 least developed countries (LDCs), while the US$2 international poverty line corresponds to the median poverty line of 75 developing economies. The national poverty lines are based on the estimated cost of a basket of basic consumption goods, which are typically anchored to minimum nutrition requirements. See Ravallion et al., 2008.

Falling labour shares and equitable growth

19 These include the previous two editions of the Global Wage Report (ILO, 2008a, 2010a); European Commission, 2007; IMF, 2007; World Bank, 2011; OECD, 2011, 2012a; UNCTAD, 2011 and 2012; and IILS, 2011, 2012, to mention but a few. In the case of studies that deal with the effect of wage share on aggregate macroeconomic components, studies such as those by UNCTAD (2011) show that much of the research on the topic so far has been in the form of descriptive correlations as opposed to estimates of the causal empirical framework we present in the current report.

20 These empirical findings date back to the early twentieth century, when Arthur Bowley first observed such regularity using British data from the nineteenth and twentieth centuries and formulated "Bowley's Law". Paul Douglas made a similar finding regarding the labour share in the United States, and developed, together with the mathematician Charles Cobb, the famous Cobb–Douglas production function, which simplifies economic modelling by assuming that the functional income distribution between labour and capital always remains constant (see Mankiw, 2003). Keynes described this empirical constancy as "a bit of a miracle" (Keynes, 1939) and later Solow questioned the reliability of the empirical evidence (Solow, 1958) (see La Marca and Lee, forthcoming).

21 Roughly, the (non-adjusted) labour income share is equal to the total compensation of employees divided by GDP, while the adjusted labour income share assumes that self-employed workers have similar average earnings to employees and adds this element to the total compensation of labour. There are advantages and disadvantages in using this standard adjustment methodology. On the one hand, the reality of self-employment is different in different types of economies: in advanced economies the self-employed are more likely to be in the formal sector and their remunerations are likely to be above that of their counterfactual employees, thus the adjusted labour share probably underestimates the true labour share. The opposite is the case for less developed economies where the self-employed are more likely to be vulnerable workers with remunerations below that of their counterfactuals in the formal sector. At the same time, however, failing to adjust the labour share for the self-employed workers leads to a significant underestimation of the actual share of GDP going to workers in the form of employment-related income. In addition, trends (the main focus of our analysis) do not change significantly when different adjustments are applied (see ILO, 2010a). Use of the adjusted labour share also provides for a consistent benchmark with most other studies.

22 The World Top Income database is available online at the Paris School of Economics at http://g-mond.parisschoolofeconomics.eu/topincomes/

23 Retained earnings are defined here as gross operating surplus minus dividend payments.

24 Federal Statistical Office, Germany, National Accounts: Domestic Product, Quarterly Results, Fachserie 18, Series 1.2, table 1.11.

25 A European Commission report concluded that "for the period for which the data is available (i.e. from the mid-1980s to early 2000s), the estimation results clearly indicate that technological progress made the largest contribution to the fall in the aggregate labour income share" (European Commission, 2007, p. 260). However, evidence is rather limited for developing countries.

26 For a description of the data sources, see Stockhammer, forthcoming.

27 In an interview with the *Financial Times* in 2007, Alan Greenspan, former President of the Federal Reserve Bank, apparently considered that the decline in the labour share and the gap between wages and productivity growth in the United States might undermine political support for free markets: see Guha (2007).

28 Aggregate demand, as noted above, is the sum of consumption, investment, net exports and government expenditures. Government consumption has been excluded from the analysis because by definition government consumption is the same as public employment income share.

29 All specific econometric results underlying the table can be found in Onaran and Galanis, forthcoming.

30 See e.g. IMF, 2012c. Note that the concept of unit labour costs as a measure of cost competitiveness is not without its critics. Felipe and Kumar consider, for example, that when unit labour costs increase, then by definition unit capital costs must decrease, and so the impact on external competitiveness is unclear (Felipe and Kumar, 2011).

31 The only advanced economy that shows zero impact on investment of an increase in profit share is the United States. In an earlier study by Onaran et al. (2011), the inclusion of interest and dividend payments in the definition of investment for the United States was found to have compounding effects that prevented the identification of the significance of an increase in capital income share (a drop in labour income share) on investment. The same may be happening in the present set of estimates. See also Hein and Vogel, 2008, who find no effects of capital income on US investment, consistent with the findings in this report.

32 One question in such a scenario would be how the incremental economic growth that might result from a lower income share would be distributed among the population. But this question is beyond the scope of the present report. For the importance of introducing the microeconomic impact of changing functional income distribution into the debate, see Atkinson, 2009.

33 Several case studies have examined this phenomenon for the United States in particular. See esp. Barba and Pivetti, 2009; Cynamon and Fazzari, 2008; Guttmann and Plihon, 2010; van Treeck Hein and Dünhaupt, 2007; and van Treeck, 2009). Econometric studies have shown that (financial and housing) wealth is a statistically significant determinant of consumption, and not only in the United States. See Ludvigson and Steindel, 1999; Mehra, 2001; Onaran, Stockhammer and Grafl, 2011; Boone and Girouard, 2002; Dreger and Slacalek, 2007.

Appendix I

34 ILO commissioned report by Farhad Mehran, Estimation of global wage trends: Methodological issues, International Labour Office, mimeo; peer reviews by Prof. Yves Tillé, Expertise report on the "Estimation of global wage trends: Methodological issues", Institute of Statistics, University of Neuchatel, mimeo; Prof. Yujin Jeong and Prof. Joseph L. Gastwirth, Comments on the draft ILO report "Estimation of global wage trends: Methodological issues", HEC Montreal and George Washington University, Washington, DC, mimeo; Dr Joyup Ahn, Responses to draft ILO report "Estimation of global wage trends: Methodological Issues", Korea Labor Institute, mimeo.

35 ILO resolution concerning the International Classification of Status in Employment (ISCE), adopted by the 15th International Conference of Labour Statisticians, Geneva, Oct. 1993.

36 ILO resolution concerning the measurement of employment-related income, adopted by the 16th International Conference of Labour Statisticians (Geneva, October 1998). http://www.ilo.org/global/What_we_do/Statistics/standards/resolutions/lang--en/docName--WCMS_087490/index.htm.

37 Aiming for the broadest possible coverage is in line with the idea that decent work and hence adequate earnings are a concern for all workers, and that statistical indicators should cover all those to whom an indicator is relevant. See ILO, 2008c.

38 We do this on the basis of the IMF's consumer price index (CPI) for the respective country. In the case of Brazil and the United States, where our national counterparts recommended the use of an alternative CPI, we relied on national sources provided by the Brazilian Institute of Geography and Statistics (IBGE) and the BLS, respectively. We also rely on the national CPI or real wage values in cases where the national statistical office of a country provides us with the data directly, or where a country's primary wage series is provided in nominal and real form.

39 Our universe includes all countries and territories for which data on employment are available from the ILO's Global Employment Trends Model (GET Model), and thus excludes some small countries and territories (e.g. the Channel Islands or the Holy See) that have no discernible impact on global or regional trends.

40 This is in line with standard survey methodology, where a model-based framework is generally used for item non-response, while a design-based framework is used for questionnaire non-response.

41 For a discussion of the missing data problem, see also ILO, 2010c, p. 8.

42 An alternative specification with GDP per capita and population size produced very similar results.

43 Data for the number of persons employed and the number of employees are from KILM, and data on GDP in 2005 PPP$ are from the World Bank's World Development Indicators.

44 The estimate, $\hat{n}_h$, of the number of employees in region h is obtained by multiplying the number of employees in countries from the region for which we have wage data with the uncalibrated weights, and then summing up across the region.

45 See e.g. the work done mainly for industrialized countries by the International Labor Comparisons programme of the US Bureau of Labor Statistics (http://www.bls.gov/fls/ [accessed 17 Sep. 2012]). Since we do not compare levels, but focus on change over time in individual countries, data requirements are less demanding in our context.

46 We estimate the number of employees in 2009 (which is not yet available from KILM) by calculating the ratio of employees over employment in 2008, and then multiplying total employment in 2009 with this ratio. The main data source for KILM is Laborsta.

47 See also ILO (2008b, p. 15) for the association between wage levels and GDP per capita. Notwithstanding this, wage developments can diverge from trends in labour productivity in the short and medium term.

Appendix II

48 OECD Glossary of statistical terms, stats.oecd.org/glossary/ [accessed 17 Sep. 2012].

Appendix III

49 The indicator government consumption as welfare indicator suggests a hump-shaped development over time: government expenditure as share of GDP peaked in the early 1980s and has followed a declining trend ever since. The role of government expenditure and the generosity of welfare spending has been highlighted previously in the literature, with emphasis on the role of the latter on the reservation wage of the working-age population; see Pierson, 1994; Korpi and Palme, 2003. Incidentally, a reduction in welfare state generosity has occurred since 1980, which is precisely the moment when the labour wage share began its downward trend. For studies that include government consumption as share of GDP to explain the falling labour wage share, see Harrison, 2002; Jayadev, 2007.

50 European Commission, 2007, and IMF, 2007, find surprisingly small, if any, effects of union density. The IMF includes union density and the tax wedge after having found no effect of other LMI variables.

51 Technological changes have also been approximated by capital–labour ratios and ICT capital or combinations of these in Bentolila and Saint-Paul, 2003, and in European Commission, 2007. The use of ICT capital (or ICT services) is a less ambiguous proxy for technological change as it reflects implemented technological change independent of the motives of its implementation.

52 In particular, such studies point to the significance of government spending and the welfare state in determining the reservation wage of participants, i.e., the level at which individuals are willing to enter the labour market. An increase in generosity (the welfare state) shifts the reservation wage upward (income effect through labour market disincentives) and therefore shifts the distribution of wages to the right, making wages higher for all: this, holding everything else constant, increases the labour income share.

53 Unemployment is expressed as the unemployment rate in the economy, and exchange rate volatility as a function of the variance of the real exchange rate. Financial reforms is based on a variable that measures entry barriers, international capital flows, interest rate controls, privatization, the development of security markets and a financial reform index. For more detail on a battery of related specifications to the baseline specification, see Stockhammer, forthcoming.

Appendix IV

54 The use of single equations in a similar aggregate demand framework has been widely used in the literature: see e.g. Onaran, 2011; Hein and Vogel, 2008; Naastepad and Storm, 2007. An alternative to the single equation approach is to estimate elasticities on a VAR system where the underlying identification restrictions are often arbitrary assumptions on the relation between consumption, investment and net exports. One advantage of using a VAR system is that of allowing for the endogeneity of the labour income share. In the single equation system the assumption of a long-run relation helps to overcome the problem of endogeneity; that is, the model assumes a stable long-run equilibrium relation in a causal framework.

55 See also Hein and Vogel, 2008: they find no effects of profit shares on US investment, consistent with the findings in this report.

56 For more details, see Onara and Galanis, forthcoming.

Bibliography

Abiad, A.G.; Detragiache, E.; Tressel, T. 2008. *A new database of financial reforms*, IMF Working Papers, 08/266. Dataset available at: http://www.imf.org/external/pubs/ft/wp/2008/Data/wp08266.zip [17 Sep. 2012].

Akyüz, Y.; Chang, H.-J.; Kozul-Wright, R. 1998. "New perspectives on East Asian development", in *Journal of Development Studies*, Vol. 34, No. 6, pp. 4–36.

Aleksynska, M.; Schindler, M. 2011. *Labor market regulations in low-, middle- and high-income countries: A new panel database,* IMF Working Paper No. 11/154 (Washington, DC). Dataset available at: http://www.imf.org/external/pubs/cat/longres.aspx?sk=25015.0 [27 Sep 2011].

Anderson, L. 2011. "Demystifying the Arab Spring: Parsing the differences between Tunisia, Egypt, and Libya", in *Foreign Affairs*, Vol. 90, No. 3 May–June, pp. 2–7.

Anspal, S.; Kraut, L.; Rõõm, T. 2010. *Sooline palgalohe Eestis: empiiriline analuus. Uuringuraport* (Gender pay gap in Estonia: empirical analysis). Eesti Rakendu-suuringute Keskus CentAR, Poliitikauuringute Keskus PRAXIS, Sotsiaalmin-isteerium. Available at: http://www.sm.ee/fileadmin/meedia/Dokumendid/V2ljaanded/Publikatsioonid/2011/Gender_pay_gap_Estonia_analysis.pdf [17 Sep. 2012].

Arandarenko, M.; Avlijas, S. 2011. "Behind the veil of statistics: Bringing to light structural weaknesses in Serbia", in V. Schmidt and D. Vaughan-Whitehead (eds): *The impact of the crisis on wages in South-East Europe* (Budapest: ILO Decent Work Technical Support Team and Country Office for Central and Eastern Europe) pp. 123–58.

Argitis, G.; Pitelis, C. 2001. "Monetary policy and the distribution of income: Evidence for the United States and the United Kingdom", in *Journal of Post Keynesian Economics*, Vol. 23, No. 4, pp. 617–38.

Artus, P. 2009. *L'équilibre macroéconomique du Monde*, Natixis Special Report No. 286 (Paris).

ASDA'A Burson-Marsteller Arab Youth Survey. 2012. "Top 10 Findings". Available at: http://www.arabyouthsurvey.com/english/ [24 Sep 2012].

Assaad, R. 1997. "The effects of public sector hiring and compensation policies on the Egyptian labor market", in *World Bank Economic Review,* Vol. 11. No. 1, Jan., pp. 85–118.

Atkinson, A. 2009. "Factor shares: The principal problem of political economy?" in *Oxford Review of Economic Policy*, Vol. 25, No. 1, pp. 3–16.

Atkinson, A.; Piketty, T.; Saez, E. 2011. "Top incomes in the long run of history", in *Journal of Economic Literature*, Vol. 49, No. 1, pp. 3–71.

Azam, M. 2009. "Changes in wage structure in urban India 1983–2004: A quantile regression decomposition", IZA Discussion Paper Series No. 3963 (Bonn), pp. 1–48.

Bacchetta, M.; Jansen, M. (eds). 2011. *Making globalization socially sustainable* (Geneva, ILO and WTO).

Bank for International Settlements (BIS). 2006. *76th Annual Report* (Basel).

Barba, A.; Pivetti, M. 2009. "Rising household debt: Its causes and macroeconomic implications – A long-period analysis", in *Cambridge Journal of Economics*, Vol. 33, No. 10, pp. 113–37.

Bassanini, A.; Duval, R. 2006. *Employment patterns in OECD Countries: Reassessing the role of policies and institutions*, OECD Economics Department Working Papers 486 (Paris, OECD).

Belser, P.; Rani, U. 2011. "Extending the coverage of minimum wages in India: Simulations from household data", in *Economic and Political Weekly*, Vol. 46, No. 22, 28 May, pp. 47–55.

Bentolila, S.; Saint-Paul, G. 2003. "Explaining movements in the labor share", in *Contributions to Macroeconomics*, Vol. 3, No. 1, pp. 1–31.

Bleaney, M. 1976. *Underconsumption theories: A history and critical analysis* (New York International Publishers).

Boily, L. 2011. "Pay premiums among major industry groups in New York City", in *Monthly Labor Review*, US Bureau of Labor Statistics, Washington, DC, Oct., pp. 22–8.

Bonnet, F.; Saget, C.; Weber, E. 2012. *Social security and minimum wage responses to the 2008 financial and economic crisis: Findings from the ILO/World Bank Inventory*, Employment Working Paper No. 113 (Geneva, ILO). Available at: http://www.ilo.org/employment/Whatwedo/Publications/working-papers/WCMS_175204/lang--en/index.htm [17 Sep. 2012].

Boone, L.; Girouard, N. 2002. *The stock market, the housing market and consumer behaviour*, OECD Economic Studies No. 35 (Paris), pp. 175–200.

Borbely, J.M. 2011. "Characteristics of displaced workers 2007–2009: a visual essay", in *Monthly Labor Review*, US Bureau of Labor Statistics, Washington, DC, Sep., pp. 3–15.

Brown, D.; Deardorff, A. 2011. "The apparel industry and the Jordanian economy: Calculating the domestic share of sector value added", paper prepared for *Better Work Jordan: Garment industry 3rd compliance synthesis report* (Geneva, ILO).

Bruno, M. 2011. *Regime de crescimento e acumulascao de capital no Brasil: Uma caracterizascao preliminar do periodo 1995–2010*, ILO Working Paper (Geneva).

Centre de Recherche et d'Etude sur la Sécurité Sociale [Tunisia]. 2011. *Enquête sur la structure des salaires Tunisie 2011,* final report, République Tunisienne/ILO, unpublished.

Crimmann, A.; Wiessner, F.; Bellmann, L. 2010. *The German work-sharing scheme: An instrument for the crisis*, Conditions of Work and Employment Series No. 25 (Geneva, ILO).

Cynamon, B.; Fazzari, S. 2008. "Household debt in the consumer age: Source of growth – risk of collapse", in *Capitalism and Society*, Vol. 3, No. 2, pp. 1–30.

Dougherty, C. 2010. "A comparison of public and private sector earnings in Jordan", Conditions of Work and Employment Series No. 24 (Geneva, ILO).

Draghi, M. 2012. "Monetary policy in unconventional times", BIS Central Bankers' Speeches, (Frankfurt am Main, European Central Bank).

Dreger, C.; Slacalek, J. 2007. "Finanzmarktentwicklung, Immobilienpreise und Konsum", in *DIW Wochenbericht*, Vol. 74, pp. 533–36.

Elbadawi, I.; Soto, R. 2011. *Fiscal regimes in and out of the MENA region*, Economic Research Forum Working Paper (Cairo).

—; —. 2012. *Resource rents, political instability and economic growth*, Economic Research Forum Working Paper (Cairo).

Epstein, G. (ed.). 2005. *Financialization and the world economy* (Cheltenham, Edward Elgar Publishing).

—; Burke, S. 2001. *Threat effects and the internationalization of production*, Political Economy Research Institute Working Paper 15 (Amherst, University of Massachusetts).

Estevão, M.; Nargis, N. 2002. *Wage moderation in France*, IMF Working Paper (Washington, DC).

European Commission (EC). 2007. "The labour income share in the European Union", in *Employment in Europe 2007*, Directorate-General for Employment, Social Affairs and Equal Opportunities (Brussels), pp. 237–72.

—. 2010. *Industrial Relations in Europe 2010*, Directorate-General for Employment, Social Affairs and Inclusion (Brussels).

—. 2012a. *Towards a job-rich recovery*, Communication from the Commission to the European Parliament, the Council, the European Economic and Social Committee and the Committee of the Regions. Available at: http://ec.europa.eu/commission_2010-2014/andor/headlines/news/2012/04/20120418_en.htm [17 Sep. 2012].

—. 2012b. AMECO: Annual macro-economic database, Directorate-General for Economic and Financial Affairs (link to dataset http://ec.europa.eu/economy_finance/ameco/user/serie/SelectSerie.cfm [17 Sep. 2012]).

—. 2012c. *Employment and Social Developments in Europe 2011* (Brussels).

Federal Statistical Office, Germany. 2009. Niedrigeinkommen und Erwerbstätigkeit (Wiesbaden), Seite 8.

—. 2012. *Volkswirtschaftliche Gesamtrechnungen, Inlandsproduktsberechnung, Lange Reihen ab 1970*, Vol. 18, No. 1.5 (Wiesbaden), table 1.8.

Feldstein, M. 2008. *Did wages reflect growth in productivity?*, NBER Working Paper Series No. 13953 (Cambridge, MA).

Felipe, J.; Kumar, U. 2011. *Unit labour costs in the eurozone: The competitiveness debate again* (Manila, Asian Development Bank).

Fleck S.; Glaser, J.; Sprague, S. 2011. "The compensation–productivity gap: A visual essay", in *Monthly Labor Review*, US Bureau of Labor Statistics, Washington, DC, Jan., pp. 57–69.

Ganguli, I.; Terrell, K. 2006. "Institutions, markets and men's and women's wage inequality: Evidence from Ukraine", in *Journal of Comparative Economics*, Vol. 34, No. 2, pp. 200–27.

Glyn, A. 2009. "Functional distribution and inequality", in W. Salverda, B. Nolan and T. Smeeding (eds): *The Oxford handbook of economic inequality* (Oxford, Oxford University Press), pp. 101–26.

Gollin, D. 2002. "Getting income shares right", in *Journal of Political Economy* (Chicago), Vol. 110, No. 2, pp. 458–74.

—. 2010. *Explaining labour's declining share of national income*, G-24 Policy Brief No. 4, Oxford University, Department of Economics.

Guha, K. 2007. "A global outlook", in *Financial Times*, 17 Sep.

Guttman, R.; Plihon, D. 2010. "Consumer debt and financial fragility", in *International Review of Applied Economics*, Vol. 24, No. 3, pp. 269–83.

Harrison, A. 2002. *Has globalization eroded labor's share? Some cross-country evidence*, mimeo, University of California at Berkeley.

Hein, E.; Mundt, M. Forthcoming. *Financialization and the requirements and potentials for wage-led recovery:A review focussing on G20 countries*, Conditions of Work and Employment . (Geneva, ILO).

—; Schoder, C. 2011. "Interest rates, distribution and capital accumulation: A post-Kaleckian perspective on the U.S. and Germany", in *International Review of Applied Economics*, Vol. 25, No. 6, pp. 693-723.

—; Vogel, L. 2008. "Distribution and growth reconsidered: Empirical results for six OECD countries", in *Cambridge Journal of Economics*, Vol. 32, No. 3, pp. 479–511.

Holman, C.; Joyeux, B.; Kask, C. 2008. "Labor productivity trends since 2000, by sector and industry", in *Monthly Labor Review*, US Bureau of Labor Statistics, Washington, DC, Feb., pp. 64–82.

Husson, M. 2010. "Le partage de la valeur ajoutée en Europe", in *La Revue de l'IRES*, Vol. 64, No.1, pp. 47–91.

International Institute for Labour Studies (IILS). 2008. *World of Work Report 2008: Income inequalities in the age of financial globalization* (Geneva, ILO/IILS).

—. 2011. *World of Work Report 2011: Making markets work for jobs* (Geneva, ILO/IILS).

—. 2012. *World of Work Report 2012: Better jobs for a better economy* (Geneva, ILO/IILS).

International Labour Office (ILO). 2008a. *Global Wage Report 2008/09: Minimum wages and collective bargaining – Towards policy coherence* (Geneva).

—. 2008b. *ILO Declaration on social justice for a fair globalization* (Geneva).

—. 2008c. *Measurement of decent work*, Discussion Paper for the Tripartite Meeting of Experts on the Measurement of Decent Work, Geneva, 8–10 Sep.

—. 2009. *Recovering from the crisis: A Global Jobs Pact* (Geneva).

—. 2010a. *Global Wage Report 2010/11: Wage policies in times of crisis* (Geneva).

—. 2010b. *Global Wage Report 2010/11: Africa brief* (Geneva).

—. 2010c. *Trends econometric models: A review of the methodology* (Geneva).

—. 2010d. *Decent work country profile: Tanzania (mainland)* (Geneva).

—.2010e. *World Social Security Report 2010/11: Providing coverage in times of crisis and beyond* (Geneva).

—. 2011a. *Working time in the twenty-first century*, Report for Discussion at the Tripartite Meeting of Experts on Working-time Arrangements, Conditions of Work and Employment Programme, TMEWTA/2011 (Geneva).

—. 2011b. *Remuneration in domestic work*, Domestic Work Policy Brief 1, Conditions of Work and Employment Branch (Geneva).

—. 2011c. *Key Indicators of the Labour Market* (*KILM*), 7th edn (Geneva).

—. 2011d. *Decent work country profile: Ukraine* (Geneva).

—. 2011e. *Panorama Laboral 2011. América Latina y el Caribe* (Lima, ILO Regional Office).

—. 2012a. *Global Employment Trends 2012: Preventing a deeper jobs crisis* (Geneva).

—. 2012b. *Decent Work Indicators: Concepts and definitions, 1st version*, May (Geneva).

—; International Finance Corporation. 2012. *Better Work Jordan: Garment industry 3rd compliance synthesis report* (Geneva, ILO).

—; World Bank. 2012. *Inventory of policy responses to the financial and economic crisis: A joint synthesis report* (Geneva and Washington, DC).

International Monetary Fund (IMF). 2007. "The globalization of labor", in *World Economic Outlook, April2007: Spillovers and cycles in the world economy* (Washington, DC), pp. 161–92.

—. 2009. *World Economic Outlook, April 2009: Crisis and recovery* (Washington, DC).

—. 2010. *World Economic Outlook, April 2010: Rebalancing growth* (Washington, DC).

—. 2012a. *World Economic Outlook, April 2012: Growth resuming, dangers remain* (Washington, DC).

—. 2012b. *World Economic Outlook, October 2012: Coping with high debt and sluggish growth* (Washington, DC).

—. 2012c. *The IMF's advice on labor market issues*, IMF Factsheet. Available at: http://www.imf.org/external/np/exr/facts/pdf/labor.pdf [17 Sep. 2012].

Jayadev, A. 2007. "Capital account openness and the labour share of income", in *Cambridge Journal of Economics*, Vol. 31, No. 3, pp. 423–43.

Jetin, B. 2012. "Distribution of income, labour productivity and competitiveness: Is the Thai labour regime sustainable?", in *Cambridge Journal of Economics,* Vol. 36, No. 4, pp.895—917.

Kapsos, S.; Horne, R. 2011. "Working poverty in the world: Introducing new estimates using household survey data", in ILO: *Key Indicators of the Labour Market*, 7th edn (Geneva, ILO), Ch. 1A.

Kerr, C. 1977. *Labor markets and wage determination: The balkanization of labor markets and other essays* (Berkeley, University of California Press).

Keynes, M. 1939. "Relative movements of real wages and output", in *Economic Journal*, Vol. 49, No. 193, pp. 34–49.

Korpi, W.; Palme, J. 2003. "New politics and class politics in the context of austerity and globalization: Welfare state regress in 18 countries, 1975–95", in *American Political Science Review*, Vol. 97, No. 3, pp. 425–46.

Krueger, A. 1999. "Measuring labor's share", in *American Economic Review*, Vol. 89, No. 2, pp. 45–51.

Kulikov, G.; Blyzniuk, V. 2010. *Impact of the financial and economic crisis on wages, income distribution and the tax system* (Budapest: ILO Decent Work Technical Support Team and Country Office for Central and Eastern Europe).

Kumhof, M.; Rancière, R. 2011. *Inequality, leverage and crises*, IMF Technical Report (Washington, DC).

La Marca, M.; Lee, S. Forthcoming. "Wages and growth in open economies: A policy dilemma?", in I. Islam and D. Kucera (eds): *Inclusive growth and structural transformation* (Basingstoke, Palgrave Macmillan and Geneva, ILO).

Lane, P.R.; Milesi-Ferretti, G.M. 2007. "The external wealth of nations mark II: Revised and extended estimates of foreign assets and liabilities, 1970–2004", in *Journal of International Economics*, Vol. 73, No. 2, pp. 223-250. Available at: http://www.imf.org/external/pubs/ft/wp/2006/data/update/wp0669.zip [15 Feb 2011].

Lavoie, M.; Stockhammer, E. Forthcoming. *Wage-led growth: concept, theories and policies*, Conditions of Work and Employment Series No. 41 (Geneva, ILO).

Lazonick, W.; O'Sullivan, M. 2000. "Maximising shareholder value: A new ideology for corporate governance", in *Economy and Society*, Vol. 29, No. 1, pp. 13–35.

Lee, S. 2012. "Varieties of minimum wage systems: Through the lens of indicator-based country rankings", in *International Labour Review*, Vol. 51, No. 3, pp. 261–74.

Lindenboim, J.; Kennedy, D.; Graña, J.M. 2011. " Wage share and aggregate demand: Contributions for labour and macroeconomic policy", paper delivered at Regulating for Decent Work Conference, ILO, Geneva, July 6-8.

Low Pay Commission. 2012. *National minimum wage: Low Pay Commission Report 2012* (Norwich, The Stationery Office).

Ludvigson, S.; Steindel, C. 1999. "How important is the stock market effect on consumption?", in *Federal Reserve Bank of New York Economic Policy Review*, July, pp. 29–51.

Luebker, M. 2011. "Labour productivity", in T. Sparreboom and A. Albee, eds: *Towards decent work in sub-Saharan Africa: Monitoring MDG Employment Indicators* (ILO, Geneva).

Lukiyanova, A. 2011. *Effects of minimum wages on the Russian wage distribution*, Working Paper in the Basic Research Program 09/EC/2011 Series: Economics (Moscow, National Research University, Higher School of Economics).

McKenzie, R.; Brackfield,D. 2008. *The OECD system of unit labour costs and related indicators*, OECD Statistics Working Paper 2008/04 (Paris).

Mankiw, N.G. 2003. *Macroeconomics*, 5th edn (New York, Worth Publishers).

Mehra, Y.P. 2001. "The wealth effect in empirical life-cycle aggregate consumption equations", in *Federal Reserve Bank of Richmond Economic Quarterly*, Vol. 87, No. 2, pp. 45–68.

Messenger, J.C. 2009. *Work sharing: A strategy to preserve jobs during the global jobs crisis*, TRAVAIL Policy Brief No. 1 (Geneva, ILO).

—; Rodriguez, S. 2010. *New developments in work sharing in middle-income countries*, TRAVAIL Policy Brief No. 2 (Geneva, ILO).

—; Ghosheh, N. (eds). 2010. *Offshoring and working conditions in remote work* (Geneva, ILO; Basingstoke, Palgrave Macmillan).

Naastepad, C.W.M.; Storm, S. 2007. "OECD demand regimes (1960–2000)", in *Journal of Post Keynesian Economics*, Vol. 29, No. 2, pp. 211–46.

Obstfeld, M.; Rogoff, K. 2009. "Global imbalances and the financial crisis: Products of common causes", MS, University of California at Berkeley.

Onaran, Ö. 2011. "Globalisation, macroeconomic performance and distribution", in E. Hein and E. Stockhammer (eds), *A modern guide to Keynesian macroeconomics and economic policies* (Cheltenham, Edward Elgar).

—; Galanis, G. Forthcoming. *Is aggregate demand wage-led or profit-led? National and global effects*, Conditions of Work and Employment Series No. 40 (Geneva, ILO).

—; Stockhammer, E.; Grafl, L. 2011. "Financialization, income distribution, and aggregate demand in the US", in *Cambridge Journal of Economics*, Vol. 35, No. 4, pp. 637–66.

Organisation for Economic Co-operation and Development (OECD). 2001. "Measuring productivity: Measurement of aggregate and industry-level productivity growth", in *OECD Manual* (Paris).

—. 2008. *OECD Employment Outlook 2008* (Paris).

—. 2011. *Divided we stand: Why inequality keeps rising* (Paris).

—. 2012a. *Inequality in labour income: What are its drivers and how can it be reduced?*, OECD Economic Department Policy Notes No. 8 (Paris).

—. 2012b. *OECD Employment Outlook 2012* (Paris).

Oya, C. 2010. *Rural inequality, wage employment and labour market formation in Africa: Historical and micro-level evidence*, Policy Integration Department Working Paper No. 97 (Geneva, ILO).

Pastore, F.; Verashchagina, A. 2004. *The distribution of wages in Belarus*, Discussion Paper No. 1140, Institute for the Study of Labour (Bonn).

Pierson, P. 1994. *Dismantling the welfare state? Reagan, Thatcher, and the politics of retrenchment* (Cambridge, Cambridge University Press).

Piketty, T.; Saez, E. 2003. "Income inequality in the United States, 1913–1998", in *Quarterly Journal of Economics*, Vol. 118 , No. 1, pp. 1–39.

Rani, U.; Belser P. 2012. "The effectiveness of minimum wages in developing countries: The case of India", in *International Journal of Labour Research*, Vol. 4, No. 1, pp. 45–66.

Ravallion, M.; Chen, S.; Sangraula, P. 2008. *Dollar a day revisited*, World Bank Policy Research Working Paper 4620 (Washington, DC).

Rizzio, M. 2011. *Rural wage employment in Rwanda and Ethiopia: A review of the current policy neglect and a framework to begin addressing it*, Policy Integration Department Working Paper No. 103 (Geneva, ILO).

Rodrik, D. 1997. *Has globalization gone too far?* (Washington, DC, Institute of International Economics).

—. 1999. "Democracies pay higher wages", in *Quarterly Journal of Economics*, Vol. 114, No. 3, pp. 707–38.

Roine, J.; Waldenström, D. 2012. "On the role of capital gains in Swedish income inequality", in *Review of Income and Wealth*, Vol. 58, No. 3, pp. 569–87.

Rossman, P. 2009. *Financialization and casualization of labour – building a trade union and regulatory response*, paper presented at the Global Labour University Conference, Mumbai, Feb.

Russian Federation Federal State Statistics Service. 2011. *Statistical Yearbook: Socio-economic indicators of the Russian Federation in 1991–2010*, annex. Available at: http://www.gks.ru/wps/wcm/connect/rosstat/rosstatsite/main/publishing/catalog/statistic Collections/doc_1270707126016 [24 Sep 2012].

Särndal, C.-E.; Deville, J.-C. 1992. "Calibration estimators in survey sampling", in *Journal of the American Statistical Association*, Vol. 87, No. 418, pp. 376–82.

Schmidt, V.; Vaughan-Whitehead, D. (eds). 2011. *The impact of the crisis on wages in South-East Europe* (Budapest: ILO Decent Work Technical Support Team and Country Office for Central and Eastern Europe).

Shehata, D. 2011. "The fall of the Pharaoh: How Hosni Mubarak's reign came to an end", in *Foreign Affairs*, Vol. 90, No. 3, May–June, pp. 26–32.

Solow, R. 1958. "A skeptical note on the constancy of relative shares", in *American Economic Review*, Vol. 48, pp. 618–31.

Sommers D.; Franklin, J.C. 2012. "Employment outlook 2010–2020: Overview of projections to 2020", in *Monthly Labor Review*, US Bureau of Labor Statistics, Washington, DC, Jan., pp. 3–2000.

Soto, R.; Huauas, I. 2011. *Has the UEA escaped the oil curse?*, Economic Research Forum Working Paper (Cairo).

—; Vazquez-Alvarez, R. 2010. *The effects of short lived immigration policies (contracts) on human capital stocks (and productivity)* (Dubai, UAE, Economic Policy and Research Center, Dubai Economic Council).

Stockhammer, E. 2004. "Financialisation and the slowdown of accumulation", in *Cambridge Journal of Economics*, Vol. 28, No. 5, pp. 719–41.

—. 2009. *Determinants of functional income distribution in OECD countries*, IMK Studies 05-2009 (Düsseldorf, Hans Böckler Stiftung).

—. Forthcoming. *Why have wage shares fallen? A panel analysis of the determinants of functional income distribution*, Conditions of Work and Employment Series No. 35. (Geneva, ILO).

Syrian Arab Republic, Central Bureau of Statistics. 2011a. *Labour Force Survey*. Available at: http://www.cbssyr.org/index-EN.htm [24 Sept 2012].

—. 2011b. *Statistical Abstract*. Available at: http://www.cbssyr.org/index-EN.htm [24 Sept 2012].

Tillé, Y. 2001. *Théorie des sondages: Echantillonage et estimation en populations finies* (Paris, Dunod).

United Nations Industrial Development Organization (UNIDO). 2006. Industrial Statistics Database. Available at: http://dx.doi.org/10.5257/unido/indstat3/2006 [15 Feb 2011].

United Nations Conference on Trade and Development (UNCTAD). 2011. *Trade and Development Report 2011* (Geneva and New York, United Nations). Available at: http://unctad.org/en/docs/tdr2011_en.pdf [17 Sep. 2012].

—. 2012. *Trade and Development Report, 2012* (Geneva and New York, United Nations). Available at: http://unctad.org/en/PublicationsLibrary/tdr2012_en.pdf [24 Sep. 2012].

United Nations Statistics Division. Various years. UN National Accounts Official Country Data, UNData Explorer. Available at: http://data.un.org/Explorer.aspx-?d=SNA

United States Department of Labor, Bureau of Labor Statistics (BLS). 2011. "International comparisons of hourly compensation costs in manufacturing, 2010", news release. Available at: http://www.bls.gov/news.release/pdf/ichcc.pdf [17 Sep. 2012].

—. 2012. "The recession of 2007–2009", in *Spotlight on Statistics*. Available at: http://www.bls.gov/spotlight/2012/recession/ [17 Sep. 2012].

Van Treeck, T. 2009. "The political economy debate on 'financialisation': A macroeconomic perspective", in *Review of International Political Economy*, Vol. 16, No. 5, pp. 907–44.

—; Hein, E.; Dunhaupt, P. 2007. *Finanzsystem und wirtschaftliche Entwicklung: Neuere Tendezen in den USA und in Deutschland*, IMK Studies 5/2007 (Düsseldorf: Hans Böckler Stiftung).

Vaughan-Whitehead, D. (ed.). 2011. *Work inequalities in the crisis: Evidence in Europe* (Cheltenham, Edward Elgar, and Geneva, ILO).

— (ed.). 2010. *The minimum wage revisited in the enlarged EU* (Cheltenham, Edward Elgar and Geneva, ILO).

Vazquez-Alvarez, R. 2012a. *Labor markets in Dubai: Main Dubai versus free zones* (Dubai, UAE, Dubai Economic Council).

—. 2012b. *Assessing the effect of the new labor market regulations for Dubai* (Dubai, UAE, Economic Policy and Research Center).

Wolff, E.; Zacharias, A. 2009. "Household wealth and the measurement of economic well-being in the United States", in *Journal of Economic Inequality*, Vol. 7, No. 2, pp. 83–115.

World Bank. 2011. *Migration and Remittances Factbook, 2011* (Washington, DC).

—. 2012. *World Development Report 2013: Jobs* (Washington, DC).

Zhou, M.; Xiao, W.; Yao, X. 2010. *Unbalanced economic growth and uneven national income distribution: Evidence from China*, Institute for Research on Labor and Employment Working Paper 2010–11 (Los Angeles, University of California Los Angeles).